THE PRACTITIONER

Marilyn Cochran-Smith and Susan L. Lytle, SERIES EDITORS

(continued)

Promising Pedagogies for Teacher Inquiry and Practice

Teaching Out Loud

EDITED BY

Katherine Crawford-Garrett
Damon R. Carbajal

Foreword by Gerald Campano

TEACHERS COLLEGE PRESS
TEACHERS COLLEGE | COLUMBIA UNIVERSITY
NEW YORK AND LONDON

Published by Teachers College Press,® 1234 Amsterdam Avenue, New York, NY 10027

Copyright © 2023 by Teachers College, Columbia University

Library of Congress Cataloging-in-Publication Data is available at loc.gov

ISBN 978-0-8077-6778-8 (paper)
ISBN 978-0-8077-6779-5 (hardcover)
ISBN 978-0-8077-8144-9 (ebook)

Printed on acid-free paper
Manufactured in the United States of America

Contents

PART III: CONCEPTUALIZING KEY TENETS OF
CRITICAL TEACHER INQUIRY

Foreword

Interdependence in Teacher Learning and Leadership

What I found was a need for collectivism.

—Kahlil Simpson

The year that I was, perhaps, at my best in classroom teaching was also the year that I grappled with a crisis of pessimism about the education system. It was around 1998, a period in my life—I was in my twenties—when I could devote many of my waking hours to crafting and enacting a curriculum, inspired by the field of critical ethnic studies, that strove to honor the histories and intellectual legacies of my 5th-graders in California's Central Valley. According to the state-sanctioned metrics of the high-stakes exams, my classroom was succeeding. More importantly, many of my students were thriving by my own evaluative standards: They had written and performed multilingual plays animated by the local political theatre, Teatro Campesino; penned historical fiction novellas on the Philippine-American War; learned 8th-grade algebra; published their own award-winning poetry inspired by June Jordan and Langston Hughes; investigated the lives of Valley icons such as Dolores Huerta and Maxine Hong Kingston; interviewed their families about their migration stories; and had created a nurturing and supportive intellectual community. My efforts were even recognized by the district. So what was the problem?

For one, I was plagued by internal doubts about individual children I had not adequately reached. But I also worried for all my students. They would enter a middle school which was, it was becoming clear to me, an extension of the carceral state, with a crushing police presence but inadequate nurses, counselors, and advanced placement classes. Despite my students' demonstrated brilliance, they were trying to survive an unconscionably underresourced system designed to dehumanize them. The test scores, the Teacher of the Year awards, it all felt like a sham: window dressing for deeper forms of oppression that permeated almost every aspect of schooling. As a teacher, isolated in my classroom, I didn't know what else to do. Despite the genuine joys and rewards of learning alongside the children and their families, I harbored a general malaise that would eventually manifest itself in acute physical and emotional duress, which at the time I kept to myself. I wish I had a colleague back then, such as Damon Carbajal—a co-editor and author of this book—who understood the necessity of "self-care for educators by educators."

Looking back, I realize that in my professional life I had not fully absorbed one of the most important lessons of critical ethnic studies and other movements for social liberation and education justice: the value, as Kahlil Simpson elegantly reminds us in this volume, of the collective in teacher learning and leadership. While I did my best to nurture community in my classroom, I was unable to organize with other educators in the school and district to engage in collective intellectual activist projects. I had been exposed to rich models of collaborative teacher inquiry, such as the National Writing Project, and had kindred spirits in my school. But teachers and schools were too often pitted against one another. And the education system—including higher education, as I have come to learn—is insidiously beholden to liberal bourgeois ideologies that suggest that through exertions of individual will, grit, talent, charisma, or innovation, one can change the world, or the world will at least self-organize according to "merit"—a recipe for exploitation and social reproduction.

Real change and real liberation, in education and in the world, is the result of the difficult, messy, day-to-day work of everyday people coming together in solidarity for justice. This requires an ethos of interdependence, not merely independence, where an individual's flourishing is intimately bound with the flourishing of the community. It has been part of my own professional journey to realize that an ethos of interdependence is our inheritance and can be mobilized in our work as educators. This ethos sustained my ancestors through centuries of colonization in Mindanao, and it enabled my father and grandparents to endure the Great Depression while staying with multiple Filipinx families across New York City during a period of housing insecurity and a resurgence of anti-Asian violence. It is the inheritance of so many of our students, especially those most marginalized in the school system (Ghiso, 2016). And it is also the inheritance of contemporary teachers, such as those who gifted us with their scholarship in this groundbreaking volume, *Promising Pedagogies for Teacher Inquiry and Practice*.

The teacher-researcher-writer-activists represented in this book embody the latest generation of the Teacher Research Movement (Cochran-Smith & Lytle, 2009), and they have much to share with the field about nurturing and sustaining collective educational projects. They remind us that teaching is, in many ways, an impossible job. One of its fundamental contradictions is that schools have historically played a central role in the oppression of Black, Brown, Immigrant, Native, and low-income students. At the same time, many families still retain deep emotional investments in education as one pathway for individual and community empowerment. Navigating the tensions of working within/against these systems, the *Teaching Out Loud* teacher inquiry community is cleared-eyed about what the writer and cultural critique Elaine Castillo (2022) characterizes as the "triumvirate of horrors" of our nation's founding genocides, including settler colonialism, enslavement, and imperial wars. The first chapters powerfully hxstoricize teaching and learning in New Mexico. It also reveals how new permutations of colonial empiricist logic drive punitive educational policies and practices, including the standardization of curriculum and surveillance and subsequent ranking of schools, teachers, youth, and by implication communities.

A precondition for genuine solidarity in teacher collective work is thus a commitment to, in the words of the Zinn Education Project, #TeachTruth. By virtue of being human, we all have a situated relationship with what several of the authors characterize as the role that forced assimilation, colonialism, white supremacy, and English-only policies have played in perpetuating educational inequalities in New Mexico and beyond. These bedrock realities become the basis for a recognition of our fundamental connections to one another, with the pandemic providing yet another reminder of our shared but unequally distributed precarities and interlocking fates. It is a methodological strength of teacher research, I believe, to recognize that there are no neutral or ideologically pure locations from which to engage in inquiry.

Unlike the isolation of my early teaching years, the *Teaching Out Loud* inquiry community has brought together an intergenerational and interracial group of educators who are creating, alongside one another, both individual and collective visions of how teaching and learning may be transformed in their respective sites of practice. In resistance to top-down mandates that, too often, emphasize the dissemination of discrete skills, they are investigating the role of play in the early childhood curriculum, fostering kindness with second graders, confronting race through culturally relevant pedagogy, exploring abolitionist teaching, and reminding us of the importance of joy and self-care in the work of education. They are restoring a fuller sense of humanity to both teaching and teacher education. At the same time, these courageous, elegantly composed chapters do not shy away from exposing the authors' own classroom vulnerabilities, dissonances, and questions, and intentionally diverge from triumphant narratives of teacher mastery and success. They model the types of fallibility and humility required for epistemic growth, trust, and collective action.

There is one final ingredient to fostering an ethos of interdependence in teacher learning evident, although subtly, throughout the chapters. I have a sense that all the researchers cherish one another. Several authors testified to the power of the *Teaching Out Loud* inquiry community, and Damon Carbajal characterized the research collaboration as a *familia*, a term that I know is not invoked lightly. This form of intimacy, involving a love that embraces difference and interdependence, is necessary for the teacher activists who, in addition to teaching their classrooms, have also gone public to various audiences—of administrators, policymakers, preservice teachers, state officials—to demand better conditions for themselves and their students. This form of collaborative research requires both significant time and relational and emotional labor.

If I have one wish for the *Teaching Out Loud* community, it is to expand their circle of inquiry to include the other educators of their students' lives: the students' parents, caretakers, families, and neighborhood leaders. For the past decade, my colleagues and I have been involved in a project where families have been engaged in original research on educational access and justice (Ghiso et al., 2022). They are ready to share their findings and be in dialogue with school-based educators because, as one of our community elders put it, "We are one and need to work together for our children's futures." Imagine what might be possible if—through collaborative inquiry—we not only break down the barriers between classroom walls, but also the ones between schools and communities. Imagine if we all teach, research, and advocate for our children, youth, and ourselves, out loud and together.

—*Gerald Campano*

REFERENCES

Castillo, R. (2022). *How to read now.* Viking Press.

Cochran-Smith, M. & Lytle, S. (2009). *Inquiry as stance: Practitioner inquiry for the next generation.* Teachers College Press.

Ghiso, M. P. (2016). The Laundromat as the transnational local: Young children's literacies of interdependence. *Teachers College Record, 118*(1), 1–46.

Ghiso, M. P., Campano, G., Thakurta, A., & Vazquez Ponce, O. (2022). Community-based research with immigrant families: Sustaining an intellectual commons of care, resistance, and solidarity in an urban intensive context. *Urban Education.* https://doi.org/10.1177/00420859221082676

Acknowledgments

We want to acknowledge the guidance received from Marsha Pincus, who helped to conceptualize and implement *Teaching Out Loud* in its initial year. She continued to serve as a thinking partner throughout.

We also want to acknowledge the Philadelphia Foundation and the University of New Mexico, as these organizations provided us with important seed money that allowed teachers to purchase curricular resources and to be compensated for their time and commitment to our inquiry community.

In addition, we want to thank Dr. Susan Lytle and Dr. Marilyn Cochran-Smith, whose research and theory of teacher inquiry has profoundly shaped our own understandings and perspectives.

Lastly, we dedicate this book to all the teachers who worked so tirelessly during the pandemic to keep learning going and who were, in turn, praised and then vilified. We recognize that our group is one small iteration of the revolutionary work being done by teachers all over the United States to create more equitable conditions in schools. This book is for them.

Promising Pedagogies for Teacher Inquiry and Practice

Introduction

Katherine Crawford-Garrett

There is no doubt that educators across the United States are teaching in contentious times. Faced with increasing political polarization, divisive politics, school shootings, debates over the role of critical race theory in schools and classrooms, concerns over climate change and environmental destruction, and the mental health fallout from the COVID-19 pandemic, to name but a few, teachers today face a monumental set of challenges. We developed and sustained *Teaching Out Loud*, a multigenerational teacher inquiry group within and against this sociopolitical backdrop, as we attempted to explore what it means to teach for social justice within and against social and political contexts that often devalue our expertise as educators. In doing so, we offer a place-based account of our work in the American Southwest, a region that is rife with the intergenerational effects of colonialism, language erasure, and a wholly unique set of policy issues and concerns that are markedly distinct from the rest of the country.

To comprehensively document our inquiries, we have organized this volume into three sections with frameworks of social justice and teacher inquiry woven throughout as key threads within the text. Part I offers a detailed account of educational policy in New Mexico over the past two decades with consideration to how it has (re)shaped teachers' work and documents the emergence of *Teaching Out Loud* to illustrate the sociopolitical origins of the group and the development of its inquiry protocols and processes. The first chapter begins with a narrative vignette from a *Teaching Out Loud* meeting in order to offer a snapshot into how the group functions, its role in the professional growth of the teacher participants, and how the group has grappled with the massive educational disruption that has resulted from COVID-19. This vignette serves as a segue to a brief discussion of the teacher research movement and the ways in which inquiry frameworks can offer educators adaptable ways to respond to troubling, dissonant, or unexpected instances that surface within broader sociopolitical contexts as well as within localized circumstances. We also discuss the ways in which critical literacy theory has shaped our ongoing work and make connections between critical literacies and the ways in which the group consistently problematizes policies and practices in the interest of creating more equitable educational conditions for students.

Chapter 2 documents the origins of *Teaching Out Loud* as a professional development initiative and shares the ways in which the group functions as an inquiry community. *Teaching Out Loud* centers on the voices of educators in designing their professional learning experiences across dimensions of difference, including race, class, gender, ethnicity, sexuality, and, most notably, experience as educators. As such, the group represents an intergenerational group of novice and experienced teachers who utilize practitioner inquiry and participatory action research to collectively explore efforts to introduce critical, creative approaches into elementary and secondary classrooms in ways that advance equity.

The group formed in the aftermath of the 2016 presidential election and the ensuing issues that surfaced in schools and universities with an initial mission to consider what it means to teach in contentious times. This chapter documents both the origin and the evolution of the group while recounting the inquiry protocols and processes the group has adopted and refined over the past 3 years. We also discuss group membership and how our intersectional identities have shaped our protocols, shared reading, curriculum development, priorities, and practices.

Chapter 3 addresses the opportunities and challenges faced by New Mexico over the past several decades as a result of the intergenerational legacies of colonialism as well as rampant neoliberal reform efforts that have included contentious policy interventions like school grading, punitive teacher evaluation systems, the expansion of charter schools, and substantial shifts in district and state leadership, alongside pervasive media depictions of the state as poor and underperforming. These challenges are presented alongside an account of the landmark lawsuit (*Yazzie/Martinez v. State of New Mexico*) that has forced the state to confront the persistent underfunding of education and endemic racial inequities. By detailing this backdrop, our goal is twofold: we consider the conditions that have contributed to decreases in teacher agency over time and a professional development culture in New Mexico focused on compliance and standardization, while also illustrating the profound possibilities for transformation in light of the renewed statewide focus on equity. Lastly, we discuss both district and state-level responses to COVID-19 and how this response has shaped teacher and student experiences in schools. Specifically, we examine the challenges that virtual learning present in New Mexico and detail the ways in which state and district agencies have attempted to ensure access in spite of significant roadblocks.

The second section of the text includes five chapters written in the voices of the educators who participate in *Teaching Out Loud*. The chapters represent the teachers' unique positionalities and divergent grade-level contexts by documenting their individual inquiries over a 2-year period and during the COVID-19 pandemic. Teachers draw on data from their classrooms and from inquiry group meetings to illustrate the challenges and opportunities presented by the pandemic, the role of *Teaching Out Loud* in supporting their development as educators, and the ways in which critical content and pedagogical practice can be incorporated into the classroom, even in high-accountability contexts. Ultimately, this section illustrates how the group itself supported teachers in re-envisioning their work as educators in light of the massive educational shifts caused by COVID-19.

In Chapter 4, Linnea Holden, a kindergarten teacher, reintroduces play as an integral part of the learning environment through manipulatives, building materials, and other creative resources. By offering little direction or explicit guidance to the students, Linnea documents through photos and observation the kind of learning that happens when young children are offered increased freedom to explore. Moreover, this chapter illustrates the kind of critical reflection that can evolve from sustained teacher inquiry as Linnea increasingly recognizes the robust funds of knowledge her students bring to the classroom as fully formed human beings. Lastly, this chapter documents the shift that occurred in kindergarten instruction as a result of virtual learning, the challenges of creating a virtual space that is inclusive and responsive to the foremost needs of the child and family during an extraordinarily contentious time.

Next, Kris Heighberger-Ortiz documents her work as a 2nd-grade teacher in Chapter 5 as she aims to deepen social-emotional learning in her classroom, foster relationships, and promote kindness among students of differing racial, ethnic, and socioeconomic backgrounds. Through co-constructing a unit that culminated in the creation of a "buddy bench," students reflect on what it means to be a good friend and to support one another in the classroom. As a result of virtual learning, Kris must reconceptualize how to do community-building work in the classroom that can promote and sustain relationships over space and time.

In Chapter 6, Amanda Short, a 4th-grade teacher, explores the role that hxstorical racism and national bias played in New Mexico's path to statehood, connecting this time period to our current state of affairs. Through hxstorical texts, oral hxstories, and personal accounts, students examine citizenship and personal identity and how this has shaped New Mexico over space and time. The challenges of virtual learning brought a new focus on culturally relevant social-emotional learning. Throughout, Amanda prompts students to reflect on their cultural identities while struggling with her own identity as a White, middle-class teacher within and against the sociopolitical backdrop of the Black Lives Matter movement.

Kahlil Simpson, a 6th- and 7th-grade language arts teacher, discusses how he navigates the obstacles and limitations presented in remote teaching in Chapter 7 of this volume. Using narrative inquiry, Kahlil examines how school structures can be read, named, and re-envisioned in light of equity and social justice. The chapter details curricular and pedagogical decision-making and highlights a shift from whitewashed and martyrdom-laden practice towards abolition and joy.

Lastly, in Chapter 8, Damon Carbajal, a community educator, examines the concept of self-care. In particular, Damon considers what it means to provide educators with intentional spaces aimed at promoting growth through holistic and authentic self-care. With an emphasis on intersectionality, social justice, and identity development, this exploration is a critique of traditional professional development. Thus, this chapter calls into question educator well-being, notions of equity in professional development, and how these elements impact students in the classroom and virtual learning spaces.

Taken collectively, these chapters focus on how teachers implemented critical curricular approaches with students before and during COVID-19 and how their participation in *Teaching Out Loud* fostered their professional development and engagement during this challenging time period, with specific attention to how the group helped the teachers maintain a commitment to their values and to justice-oriented teaching.

The final section concludes the volume with the aim of conceptualizing ways forward by highlighting key tenets that have emerged from *Teaching Out Loud*. This chapter serves as a concluding chapter by summarizing themes that surface across the inquiries and offering a conceptual framework for sustaining meaningful teacher inquiry across time and space. These tenets include (1) intergenerationality, (2) participatory processes, and (3) public dissemination. In discussing intergenerationality, we consider the importance of having a group that includes preservice teachers, early-career teachers, and more experienced educators and share specific examples of how intergenerationality contributes to the sustained inquiry and collective support that the group offers. Next, we discuss our participatory processes for research and inquiry, which we use both individually to support our own respective classroom inquiries and collectively as we inquire into the group as a whole through our collaborative research efforts.

Finally, we discuss the role of public dissemination, which is central to the mission of our group and indexed by our name—*Teaching Out Loud*—and detail specific ways in which we have made critical practices public. As we delve into each of these tenets, we draw on examples provided in the book to illustrate for the reader how these threads connect across the various inquiries. We also share our recommendations for moving critical, participatory, teacher inquiry work forward, with suggestions on how this work might be implemented across contexts with a focus on deepening teachers' professional engagement in ways that support justice and equity for all students.

One of the central goals of this text is to extend current scholarship on teacher inquiry by offering a set of conceptual tools and pedagogical practices for teacher educators and researchers seeking to advance teacher learning and leadership through the use of critical study groups rather than the more scripted professional development approaches that tend to dominate hxstorically marginalized settings. More specifically, this book demonstrates, through the voices of a diverse set of differently positioned teachers, the role teacher inquiry can have in shifting curriculum and advancing equity, even when faced with formidable circumstances like a global pandemic.

Specifically, we examine how participation in *Teaching Out Loud* helped teachers maintain their values and attend to pedagogical priorities like fostering social/emotional learning, foregrounding issues of race and identity, building and sustaining community, promoting self-care, and centering play within and against challenging contexts.

Part I

TEACHER INQUIRY IN CONTENTIOUS TIMES

CHAPTER 1

Setting the Stage

The Foundations of *Teaching Out Loud*

Katherine Crawford-Garrett

SHIFTING CONDITIONS, SHIFTING INQUIRIES: A PORTRAIT OF COMMUNITY

It is September 2020, 6 months into the COVID-19 pandemic, and our monthly meeting for *Teaching Out Loud*, a professional development (PD) community of eight educators in Albuquerque, New Mexico, gathers via Zoom. It is unseasonably hot for September. As eager as we are to connect after a summer apart, the meeting feels as heavy as the heat. Any hopes that the pandemic would subside in time for an in-person start to the 2020/2021 school year had long since faded, and teachers are struggling to make remote learning work within and against a complex sociopolitical environment shaped by inequitable Internet access, food and housing scarcity, and a dearth of district-level support for teachers. We begin our meeting with a story circle. Our goal is to create spaces that allow each participant to relate a story central to their current experience as educators, whether hopeful, contentious, or unsettling. The stories comprise a critical starting point; there will be much to navigate in the coming months.

Our prepandemic meetings were held in a cheerful conference room decorated with artifacts from our time together—symbols we had drawn by hand to represent our individual and collective vision.

We once shared snacks and coffee as we related personal and professional challenges, engaged in book discussions, and analyzed lesson plans and student work in an effort to delve deeper into practice. Our group was built on a strong foundation of teacher inquiry that centered notions of teachers and students as knowledge creators. The group had developed and evolved over a 3-year period as members joined, deepened their commitment to the group, or stepped away to pursue other opportunities or priorities. Figure 1.1 exemplifies our community building practices where we created a collective *Teaching Out Loud* mural to showcase what we as a

Figure 1.1. Each of us drew a symbol to represent a tenet of our teaching philosophy.

community of educators value in education and PD. In our nascent Zoom environment, we attempt to maintain the intimacy and trust that have developed over several years of collaboration, but we can also sense what is lost across the Internet ether.

At this September meeting, Amanda, a White 4th-grade teacher, begins our session by wondering how students will be assessed during COVID-19, a question that includes in its subtext the problematic role assessment has hxstorically played in her school, as both kids and teachers are sorted according to a troubling set of metrics: "And so that kind of brings me to the question of how can I help support school-wide change?" Amanda said. "Or how can I at least start that conversation as far as what data we are collecting." Linnea, a Hispanic, female kindergarten teacher who works at the same school as Amanda, shares the obstacles she encountered as she tried to support families whose lives had been upended by the pandemic. Recognizing that one particular mother was struggling to meet the basic needs of her daughter, Linnea shares the following: "And so I called CYFD (Children, Youth and Families Department) for the very first time to reach out for support, not to report abuse or neglect. And that was new and different. And I think it might have worked. The mom did message me this weekend and said that they were in line to get an apartment, to get approval for and funding for an apartment." Just as Amanda considers new ways to assess students, Linnea identifies innovative approaches for supporting parents. Even with all of the challenges it represented, the pandemic offered opportunities for reinvention. The pandemic had the potential to reveal the stark disparities that permeate the U.S. educational system. It also had the potential to create opportunities for society to view students and teachers differently, more holistically.

Sarah, a White 8th-grade English language arts (ELA) teacher and another member of our group, shares that her aunt had died of COVID-19 and that her cousin could not focus in school as a result. Sarah immediately uses this narrative as a means through which to reflect on her own teaching. Specifically, she wonders how she might create a space where students can say, "Hey, I can't do this today." Like Linnea and Amanda, Sarah views the pandemic as an invitation to be more responsive to the most urgent needs of her young adolescents from both within and outside of the conditions created by COVID-19. Like Sarah, Kris, a White, 2nd-grade teacher, has focused her inquiries and questions around issues of social-emotional learning. Her prepandemic project involved building a buddy bench that she envisioned as a physical space for building friendship and community. After the COVID-19 shutdown, Kris grappled with how to create spaces that could help students develop meaningful relationships with one another. In describing a recent virtual math lesson, Kris relates the following: "He just told a joke. And he thought the joke was related and the kids just went with it. So, we actually stopped math and had joke time. And it reminded me of how they tell their funny little jokes walking in from recess, and they don't get to do that now. They don't have that spontaneous talk with the teacher. So that was nice." Kris aptly recognizes the importance of liminal spaces or transition times for students and considers what happens when students no longer have these informal spaces in which to joke and laugh. She makes an in-the-moment decision during a math lesson to allow space for informal joking—it is one way she can foster a sense of community from a distance.

Though he joined our group when he was a secondary ELA teacher, Damon, a queer, Chicanx man, is pursuing an MA in Chicano/a studies and a certificate in race and social justice at the local university, where he sees firsthand the ways in which institutions continually fail their students who must navigate an emotionally fraught landscape with little support. At the September meeting, Damon recounts how his graduate student peers had contacted him as they attempted to complete their degree requirements while facing dire mental health issues. "I've had four different peers in my cohort reach out to me in a panic at like three in the morning and midnight. And I don't feel like higher ed is being flexible right now in any regard; I didn't realize how bad it was until they were calling me in panic." Damon, who consistently promotes self-care among teachers and students, wonders how some of these challenges might be mitigated within and against the backdrop of the pandemic and, like the other *Teaching Out Loud* participants, questions the responsibility of institutions to be more responsive to students.

Reflecting how important issues of self-care have become for educators, Kahlil, a Black man, who also teaches middle school ELA, details how an administrator at his school showed a series of inspirational videos at an in-service PD session. Noting that for him, they represented a kind of toxic positivity, Kahlil shares the following: "And I just think it's so insensitive to make us be positive in that setting when what would be positive for me is not wasting my time and letting me do my own self care." Kahlil identified more meaningful resources for maintaining hope during the pandemic, including the poetry of Ross Gay, who views it as an "ethical imperative to notice and articulate the way that our lives are made possible." Kahlil continuously reflects on why and how this approach to positivity feels so different than the inspirational videos introduced by the school. Like all the educators in *Teaching Out Loud*, Kahlil confronts the ways in which his personal and professional identities can conflict with institutional mandates.

Teacher inquiry is predicated on dissonance. Prior to the pandemic, participants in *Teaching Out Loud* had been individually and collectively identifying and interrogating moments of dissonance in their practice. The advent of COVID-19, however, introduced a level of dissonance that had previously been unimaginable. Yet one of the key arguments that we put forth in this volume is that the practices of teacher inquiry to which *Teaching Out Loud* participants had already become accustomed allowed these educators to face the challenges presented by the pandemic from a place of inquiry and deep curiosity as they consistently foregrounded the needs and experiences of students and families.

Kahlil, Damon, Kris, Sarah, Linnea, Amanda, and I speak and teach from different social locations, and our positionalities have informed and shaped our pedagogies, practices, and responses to the pandemic in fundamental ways. The group was cofounded and cofacilitated by me and Marsha Pincus, a retired secondary English teacher from Philadelphia who moved to New Mexico, where she continued to explore her classroom experiences through writing and performance. As facilitators and White, middle-class women who inhabit a range of privileged locations, our goal in cofounding and facilitating *Teaching Out Loud* was to amplify the voices of teachers and create meaningful space for curriculum that centered student voice in ways that the mandated curriculum did not. Throughout this volume, the voices of these educators (and those of their students) are highlighted alongside the tensions, contradictions, insights, and challenges indicative of our individual and shared inquiries into our pedagogical practice.

THE TEACHER RESEARCH MOVEMENT

Over the past 2 decades, teacher PD has increasingly mirrored the U.S. educational policy environment with a disproportionate focus on testing, curriculum implementation, and accountability with little input from teachers' themselves (Hardy & Ronnerman, 2011; Yendol-Hoppey & Dana, 2010). Specifically, "teacher professional development has become 'product implementation' aligned with standards and standardized tests and is increasingly conducted by those employed by testing companies and publishers who produce and sell the materials that are promoted by the government" (Zeichner, 2010, p. 1546). As Campano (2007) notes, accountability-driven PD assumes that "the knowledge needed to bring students up to par must be proved, imported to schools, and codified as professional development, especially in districts that serve low-income and minority populations. Prospective teachers should be 'trained' in 'scientifically-proven best practices'" (p. 3).

In essence, the onus of PD has shifted away from teachers (and even districts and states) and become corporatized in ways that significantly diminish the voices and agency of educators. Currently, teachers and administrators are increasingly "put in a position in which they must look to market and test-based forms of accountability for direction rather than their professional training, associations, or unions" (Anderson & Cohen, 2015, p. 5).

These reforms not only shape the actual delivery of PD programs but also contribute to how teachers view themselves and the profession as a whole—a phenomenon that contributes to profound tensions (Anderson & Cohen, 2015). For example, teachers in New Orleans reported "experiencing a 'moral distance' (Hargreaves, 2001) between what they believed to be right and behavior to which they were being trained and held accountable" (Sondel, 2017, p. 7). Even teacher education programs that espouse progressive approaches and justice-oriented philosophies provide mixed messages on professionalism, promoting teachers as agents of change while simultaneously discouraging the disruption of the status quo (Tolbert & Eichelberger, 2014).

In New Mexico in particular, teachers not only have very limited opportunities for PD but have increasingly faced a punitive evaluation system and a lack of autonomy (Crawford-Garrett et al., 2017), as the state now faces a record number of teacher shortages (Perea, 2018) and decreasing enrollment in teacher education programs. Despite these bleak metrics, both in New Mexico and nationwide, researchers and practitioners have documented deep, ongoing, justice-focused PD that privileges teacher research and educator agency (Colvin, 2018; Crawford-Garrett, Perez, & Short, 2016; Crawford-Garrett, Perez, Sánchez et al., 2016; Maloney et al., 2019). As Sleeter (2008) notes, "Professional development programs with the most promise combine ongoing practice-based inquiry with classroom-based learning. The venue appears to be less important than the extent to which it supportively stretches teachers beyond their existing beliefs and understandings" (p. 1951).

One prominent iteration of the kind of PD programs that Sleeter (2008) promotes involves critical teacher study groups, which, in addition to providing significant support to teachers, also serve as sites of resistance to market reforms and neoliberal interventions (Picower, 2011; Riley, 2015; Sondel, 2017). Current classroom conditions, both locally and nationally, require "the creation of *counter publics* which Fraser (1990) called 'parallel discursive arenas where members of subordinated social groups invent and circulate counter discourses, which in turn permit them to formulate oppositional interpretations of their identities, interests, and needs'" (Anderson & Cohen, 2015, p. 8). For example, in a study of critical spaces for teachers in post-Katrina New Orleans, the critical study group documented by Sondel (2017) collaborated with other local teaching and activist groups to oppose the influx of teachers like them, who were largely White and inexperienced. This collaboration allowed the teachers (most of whom had come to New Orleans via Teach for America [TFA]) to complicate their hxstorical, social, and political understanding of New Orleans—a process that involved debunking many misconceptions learned and reinforced by organizations like TFA, which had a substantial policy presence in post-Katrina New Orleans. As a result, participants were able to cultivate new identities within the group that enabled them to resist standardizing, de-professionalizing, and racist policies and narratives in schools, yet they also developed new alliances to outside organizations, connecting them to a larger network of activists, teachers, and organizers from which they were able to gain new knowledge and resources (Sondel, 2017).

COVID-19 has presented unprecedented challenges to educators across the world; however, teachers in hxstorically marginalized communities, like many of those in New Mexico, have faced especially difficult circumstances as they try to rectify educational inequities while addressing the material and emotional needs of students and families. Compounding these complexities is the context of teacher PD, which has disproportionately focused on implementation and compliance at the expense of creativity and autonomy, both in New Mexico and elsewhere (Anderson & Cohen, 2015). Social justice educators who aim to deepen their practice, foster student engagement, and foreground issues of equity must often seek out alternative spaces to supplement their professional learning. For the teachers featured in this volume, *Teaching Out Loud* filled this gap.

Drawing on frameworks of teacher research (Cochran-Smith & Lytle, 1993; Cochran-Smith & Lytle, 2009) as well as tangible examples of teacher inquiry (Campano, 2007), participatory action research (McTaggart, 1994), and critical literacy theory and practice (Janks, 2014), this volume will document the experiences of five educators in New Mexico who participate in *Teaching Out Loud*, with specific attention to how the inquiry community supported teachers to individually and collectively respond to the challenges posed by the COVID-19 pandemic in ways that allowed them to maintain their commitments to equity and social justice.

One of the primary ways that *Teaching Out Loud* aims to disrupt the cycle of oppressive PD is through the inclusion of critical literacy. Critical literacy challenges traditional PD, as it encourages educators to question notions of "best practice" and apply critical lenses to classroom curricula and pedagogy. Critical literacy requires educators to understand the school context, their personal identities, and their professional position as teachers within the larger institution while provoking questions, sharing struggles, and positing solutions (Riley, 2015). We seek to add to this body of literature by illustrating the ways in which *Teaching Out Loud* served as a space for critical, intergenerational teacher inquiry among participants and offered a means through which to disrupt mandated, top-down, and scripted PD.

Critical literacy theory and practice is centrally concerned with agency—specifically responding to social inequity and injustice in ways that can offer new social positions and societal structures that equalize opportunities for hxstorically oppressed and marginalized populations (Freire, 1970; Jones & Woglom, 2013; Luke, 2000). While societal structures can seem intractable, the social conditions in which we live are not predetermined (Janks, 2014); we create them through language and discourse. Critical literacies facilitate the recognition of how dominant discourses reproduce the status quo and reinforce long-standing disparities based on social class, race, gender, and sexuality, to name but a few. Oppression and inequality, then, are not natural occurrences; rather, they are produced collectively and individually both by our actions and by our failures to act.

Centering critical approaches to education can help us name and interrogate our practices in order to change them. *Teaching Out Loud* is predicated on this premise. As teachers co-construct knowledge, exhibit agency, question taken-for-granted practices, share student work, offer and receive emotional support, and design equity-driven curriculum, true educational transformation becomes possible.

REFERENCES

Anderson, G., & Cohen, M. I. (2015). Redesigning the identities of teachers and leaders: A framework for studying new professionalism and educator resistance. *Education Policy Analysis Archives, 23*(91), 1–27.

Campano, G. (2007). *Immigrant students and literacy: Reading, writing, and remembering.* Teachers College Press.

Cochran-Smith, M., & Lytle, S. (1993). Relationships of knowledge and practice: Teacher learning in communities. *Review of Research in Education, 24*(1), 249–305.

Cochran-Smith, M., & Lytle, S. (2009). *Inquiry as stance: Practitioner research for the next generation.* Teachers College Press.

Colvin, S. (2018). Social justice professional development. *Voice of Youth Advocates, 3,* 46.

Crawford-Garrett, K., Perez, M., Sánchez, R., Short, A., & Tyson, K. (2016). Activism IS good teaching: Reclaiming the profession. *Rethinking Schools, 30*(2), 22–25.

Crawford-Garrett, K., Perez, M., & Short, A. (2016). Leveraging literacies for social change: Portraits of teacher resistance at an "F" school. *Teaching Education, 28*(3), 227–243.

Crawford-Garrett, K., Sánchez, R., & Tyson, K. (2017). "If I give one more piece, it's gonna be the end of me": The trauma of teaching under NCLB. *Critical Education, 8*(3), 1–21.

Fraser, N. (1990). Rethinking the public sphere: A contribution to the critique of actually existing democracy. *Social Text, 25/26,* 56–80.

Freire, P. (1970). *Pedagogy of the oppressed.* Continuum.

Hardy, I., & Ronnerman, K. (2011). The value and valuing of continuing professional development: Current dilemmas, future directions and the case for action research. *Cambridge Journal of Education, 41*(4), 461–472.

Hargreaves, A. (2001). Emotional geographies of teaching. *Teacher's College Record, 103*(6), 1056–1080.

Janks, H. (2014). Critical literacy's ongoing importance for education. *Journal of Adolescent and Adult Literacy, 57*(5), 349–356.

Jones, S., & Woglom, J. (2013). Teaching bodies in place. *Teacher's College Record, 115*(8), 1–29.

Luke, A. (2000). Critical literacy in Australia: A matter of context and standpoint. *Journal of Adolescent and Adult Literacy, 43*(5), 448–461.

Maloney, T., Hayes, N., Crawford-Garrett, K., & Sassi, K. (2019). Preparing and supporting teachers for equity and racial justice: Creating culturally relevant, collective, intergenerational, co-created spaces. *Review of Education, Pedagogy and Cultural Studies, 41*(4–5), 252–281.

McTaggart, R. (1994). Participatory action research: Issues in theory and practice. *Educational Action Research, 2*(3), 313–337.

Perea, S. (2018, November 3). Large number of New Mexico teacher vacancies called a 'crisis'. *The Albuquerque Journal.* https://www.abqjournal.com/1241697/new -mexico-teacher-vacancies-called-a-crisis.html

Picower, B. (2011). Learning to teach and teaching to learn: Supporting the development of new social justice educators. *Teaching Education Quarterly, 38*(4), 7–24.

Riley, K. (2015). Enacting critical literacy in English classrooms: How a teacher learning community supported critical inquiry. *Journal of Adolescent & Adult Literacy, 58*(5), 417–425.

Sleeter, C. (2008). Equity, democracy, and neoliberal assaults on teacher education. *Teaching and Teacher Education, 24*(8), 1947–1957.

Sondel, B. L. (2017). The new teachers' roundtable: A case study of collective resistance. *Critical Education, 8*(4), 1–24.

Tolbert, S., & Eichelberger, S. (2014). Surviving teacher education: A community cultural capital framework of persistence. *Race Ethnicity and Education, 19*(5), 1–18.

Yendol-Hoppey, D., & Dana, N. F. (2010). *Powerful professional development: Building expertise within the four walls of your school.* Corwin Press.

Zeichner, K. (2010). Competition, economic rationalization, increased surveillance, and attacks on diversity: Neo-liberalism and the transformation of teacher education in the U.S. *Teaching and Teacher Education, 26*(8), 1544–1552.

CHAPTER 2

Professional Development in Contentious Times

The Origins and Practices of *Teaching Out Loud*

Damon R. Carbajal, Katherine Crawford-Garrett, and Kahlil Simpson

Teaching Out Loud was created in the aftermath of the 2016 presidential election and, as a teacher inquiry community, aimed to combat inequities by creating a shared space of activist educators. The group was cocreated by the educator-participants and the facilitator Dr. Katy Crawford-Garrett and, in turn, became an organic community where teacher inquiry, intellectual engagement, and peer support took center stage. More importantly, it represented a space that was notably absent from district-sanctioned professional development, though increasingly essential as the teaching profession faced continuous attack. Freire (2000) argues that teaching in inherently political and shifting political landscapes across the United States has made it difficult for educators to practice authentic inquiry that is based on social justice and equity. *Teaching Out Loud* was conceptualized as a community that centers on the political tensions of the profession while also emphasizing radical support and the role of humanizing pedagogies and practices (Gould, 2012). We believe these elements are essential if meaningful teaching is to become a reality in our schools.

ORIGINS OF *TEACHING OUT LOUD*

Teaching Out Loud began serendipitously when Katy connected with Marsha Pincus, a former Philadelphia public school teacher and playwright, who happened to be living and performing in Santa Fe, New Mexico. Katy attended a performance of Marsha's one-woman show, *Chalkdust*, which tells the story of a young White teacher in Philadelphia. Katy began considering how Marsha's script might be used within the context of teacher education at the University of New Mexico to help students understand the importance and complexity involved in engaging issues of race and culture in the classroom. Around the same time, Trump was elected president and, after the 2016 presidential election, a series of hate crimes occurred on the university campus, including the forcible removal of a Muslim woman's hijab in the library and swastikas being spray-painted on campus. Additionally, students came to Katy's classes sharing discussions percolating in public school classrooms as young students wrestled with Trump's immigration policies, litany of executive orders, and appointment of Betsy DeVos as education secretary. These events led Katy and several other university colleagues to create, "The Teaching in Contentious Times Conference," which was held at the University of New Mexico in the spring of 2017. (For more information on the origins of the conference, see Crawford-Garrett, Sànchez, & Meyer, 2018.) While the initial conference was a success and engaged close to 100 preservice teachers in workshops related to race, gender, and sexuality in education, among other issues, Katy (and the other organizers) did not want the conference to be a stand-alone event, recognizing that one-time events seldom lead to lasting change or create spaces where true transformation is possible. Thus, in 2018, when it was time to host the conference for a second time, Katy invited Marsha to serve as the keynote speaker and also worked with Marsha to conceptualize a fellowship program that would emerge from the conference and continue into the following year.

As part of the keynote, Marsha mapped elements of her play, *Chalkdust,* onto the theme of "contentious times." In addition to Marsha's keynote address, the *Teaching in Contentious Times Conference* included a variety of workshops for educators that centered on social justice and community-centered pedagogy. The closing session of the conference was an announcement of the *Teaching Out Loud* fellowship program as well as the opening of the application process. The funding for *Teaching Out Loud* was supported by a grant from a private foundation in its initial year and in subsequent years by the University of New Mexico. From the initial applications, an inaugural group was formed and included the seven members noted next.

TEACHING OUT LOUD MEMBERS

During the 3 years of *Teaching Out Loud,* a variety of educators moved in and out of the space. Following is an overview of participants, including a brief personal description as well as their tenure in the program (Table 2.1).

Table 2.1. *Teaching Out Loud* Participants.[1]

Year	Group Members[2]	Project	Books/Materials Read
Year 1	**Katy (she/her)** is a White, middle-class university professor, activist, and former elementary and middle school teacher and is the group facilitator.	*Teaching Out Loud* facilitator	*Immigrant Students and Literacy: Reading, Writing, and Remembering* by Gerald Campano
	Damon (he/él) is an educator, scholar, activist, and artist. He identifies as a gay, queer, Latinx, and Chicanx cisgender male originally from Las Cruces, New Mexico.	Mental Health and Musicals in the English classroom	*Pedagogy of Freedom: Ethics, Democracy, and Civic Courage* by Paulo Freire
	Kahlil (he/him) is a Black, middle-class, cisgender, male educator in Albuquerque, New Mexico.	Student-centered poetry	*None of the Above: The Untold Story of the Atlanta Public Schools Cheating Scandal, Corporate Greed and the Criminalization of Educators* by Anna Simonton and Shani Robinson
	Amanda (she/her) is a White, middle-class, veteran teacher-activist in Albuquerque, New Mexico. She is currently a 4th-grade teacher at a local public school.	Citizenship in New Mexico and Identity	
	Marsha (she/her) is an educator and writer who has been teaching English and drama and coaching writers for over 40 years.	*Teaching Out Loud* cofacilitator	
	Esther (she/her) is a White, female, 2nd-grade teacher who teaches at a dual-language elementary school that serves a hxstorically marginalized student population.	Literary Circles in a Dual Language Classroom	
	Lisa (she/her) is a Hispanic female and currently a 4th-grade teacher.	Photovoice in the Kindergarten Classroom	

(continued)

Table 2.1. (*continued*)

Year	Group Members[2]	Project	Books/Materials Read
Year 2	**Linnea (she/her)** (born and raised in New Mexico) has been working with small children for over 20 years as a babysitter, nanny, day care worker, after-school program coordinator, and public school educator.	The Importance of Play in Elementary School	*Puzzling Moments, Teachable Moments: Practicing Teacher Research in Urban Classrooms* by Cynthia Ballenger
	Kris (she/her) has been teaching in Albuquerque for the past 25 years. Her experience spans private, parochial, and public schools in Grades K–3.	Creating a Kinder Community Through a Peer Bench	*The Teacher Wars: A History of America's Most Embattled Profession* by Dana Goldstein
	Sarah (she/her) is a White, 8th-grade language arts teacher in Albuquerque, New Mexico.	Teaching/ Learning Through Trauma in Middle School	*How to Be an Antiracist* by Ibram X. Kendi
	Xiomara (she/her) is a former New Mexico Teacher of the Year. She teaches high school Spanish in Albuquerque, New Mexico.	Equitable Learning and Growth in the Spanish Classroom	
	Tamara (she/her) is a master's student at the University of New Mexico in the College of Education and Human Sciences.	Group observer and aided with translation/data collection	
	Katy (she/her) returning member	*Teaching Out Loud* facilitator	
	Damon (he/él) returning member	Educator self-care	
	Kahlil (he/him) returning member	Educator/student co-constructed poetry club	
	Amanda (she/her) returning member	New Mexico Hxstory and Identity	

(*continued*)

Table 2.1. (*continued*)

Year	Group Members[2]	Project	Books/Materials Read
Year 3	**Linnea (she/her) returning member**	Navigating Student Attendance and Participation in a Pandemic	Webinar: *Abolitionist Teaching and the Future of our Schools* by Haymarket Books (featuring Bettina L. Love, Dr. Gholnecsar (Gholdy) Muhammad, Dena Simmons, and Brian Jones)
	Kris (she/her) returning member	Creating Community in Virtual Spaces	
	Sarah (she/her) returning member	Maintaining a Productive Classroom in a Pandemic	
	Katy (she/her) returning member	*Teaching Out Loud* facilitator	
	Damon (he/él) returning member	Educator Self-Care in a Pandemic	
	Kahlil (he/him) returning member	Home Visit Impacts and Self-Care as Classroom Inquiry	
	Amanda (she/her) returning member	New Mexico Hxstory and Identity	

CRITICAL READING AS AN AVENUE FOR GROWTH

In light of the shifting membership of the group, a key component of *Teaching Out Loud* is shared readings and materials. Each semester a book or related material is selected as an anchor for our shared exploration. The book and/or materials are based on topics that we collectively felt would support us to become more culturally and social justice–oriented educators or provide skills to aid in our inquiry process. These texts also allow new educators who join the group to establish shared knowledge regarding teacher inquiry and education overall. An interesting aspect about the *Teaching Out Loud* group—and perhaps teacher inquiry groups in general—is their ability to create a liminal or third space (Stevenson & Deasy, 2005). When teachers enter into a shared inquiry within a group, the impact of that shared study not only appears in the discourse of the group but follows the teachers back to their individual contexts (i.e., their schools and classrooms). Thus, this learning provides a point of discussion and commonality across our classrooms that extends beyond the K–16 spectrum and into community spaces. Texts were often suggested by educator-participants or selected collectively to ensure that teacher voice was honored in the process.

The texts and webinars shown in Table 2.2 are complemented with a variety of resources that spanned academic journal articles to pop culture, videos, and music, as well as materials that came from each of the educator's projects. Through this varied use of materials that honor both academic and community-oriented texts, we are able to explore social justice pedagogy and teacher inquiry from a variety of angles. The books and related materials played a critical role in creating a space of resistance because it allowed us to refine what types of texts should be used in professional development and to validate the experiences and points of view from communities that

Table 2.2. Books and Related Materials.

Books and Related Materials		
Year 1	Year 2	Year 3
Immigrant Students and Literacy: Reading, Writing, and Remembering by Gerald Campano	*Puzzling Moments, Teachable Moments: Practicing Teacher Research in Urban Classrooms* by Cynthia Ballenger	Webinar: *Abolitionist Teaching and the Future of our Schools* by Haymarket Books (featuring Bettina L. Love, Dr. Gholnecsar [Gholdy] Muhammad, Dena Simmons, and Brian Jones)
Pedagogy of Freedom: Ethics, Democracy, and Civic Courage by Paulo Freire	*The Teacher Wars: A History of America's Most Embattled Profession* by Dana Goldstein	
None of the Above: The Untold Story of the Atlanta Public Schools Cheating Scandal, Corporate Greed, and the Criminalization of Educators by Anna Simonton and Shani Robinson	*How to be an Antiracist* by Ibram X. Kendi	

have been neglected in traditional academic and professional development spaces (i.e., femme, BIPOC, queer, etc.).

EMBRACING DIVERSITY TO CHALLENGE SYSTEMIC INEQUITIES

As evidenced earlier, *Teaching Out Loud* included a highly intersectional and diverse group of educators. We lean into diversity and challenge our own positionalities, knowing that doing so is necessary for promoting equitable classrooms. Specifically, we each acknowledge who we are, where we come from, and the privileges that we have and do not have. This self-reflection ensures that our professional development community is a safe space for those who come from marginalized communities (Fast, 2018; Kelly & Bhangal, 2018). We root our conversations around gender, ability, sexuality, nationality, and the intersectional identities we all inhabit (Collins & Bilge, 2016; Crenshaw, 1989). We use our differences to bridge barriers and our similarities to foster connection. For example, though only one member of the group identifies as queer, we collectively committed to using a queer lens within our work to ensure that LGBTQIA+ students have access to educational opportunities in ways that honor their sexuality and gender identity. This was not the case for many of the educators when entering the space, but because of the willingness of various group members to share their experiences and their work, it opened new insights and invited specific participants to think differently. This is just one of many examples of what *Teaching Out Loud* has offered participants both intentionally and unintentionally. It is critical to note who we are and how we developed as a collective because humanizing pedagogies (Bartolome, 1994; del Carmen Salazar, 2013; Huerta, 2011) require an understanding of one another and how people speak to and from a range of distinct sociopolitical locations.

With all this in mind, we define a *Teaching Out Loud* educator as one who is willing to challenge systems, name issues of injustice in society, and explore what it means to be human with their students even if it requires vulnerability or disrupts what society says a teacher should and should not do. Thus, we are a collective of teacher-activists, and we each use our own unique positions in and out of K–16 educational spaces to enact change and challenge systems that foster inequity.

HXSTORY OF *TEACHING OUT LOUD*

Cohort 1

Following the "Teaching in Contentious Times Conference" and the open call for educators, the first cohort convened in the fall of 2018 and consisted of two veteran teachers, Kahli, and Amanda; three preservice teachers who were in the midst of student teaching, Damon, Lisa, and Esther; the group facilitator, Katy; and a retired educator and playwright, Marsha. The first year focused on educator-participants using the allotted stipend ($500) to create a meaningful and student-centered curriculum project that could be enacted over the course of the academic year. Each project enacted social justice pedagogy in highly localized ways. The projects were spread across the K–12 continuum and uniquely situated to the expertise, context, and passions of each educator-participant. Specifically, the projects included photovoice with kindergarten students, creating spoken-word poetry with middle school students, debating New Mexico statehood in an elementary classroom, creating and enacting bilingual literature circles, and reading and interpreting modern musicals with a focus on mental health in secondary English. The wide variety of topics and materials was deeply connected to real-world issues and teaching in contentious times.

Cohort 2

In the fall of 2019, group membership shifted as preservice teachers moved into their first year of teaching and new members were recruited. The second cohort involved four of the original members and four additional members: a first-year middle school teacher, Sarah; two veteran elementary teachers, Linnea and Kris; and a secondary Spanish teacher, Xiomara. The new group of teachers followed a similar format to the first cohort, each creating a project aimed at generating curriculum that fostered equity in their classrooms. The projects this time included educator self-care, poetry as empowerment, identity-based learning, trauma pedagogy, play and its importance in the kindergarten classroom, and the role of kindness in an elementary classroom. The group had a strong racial equity lens as the focus for the shared learning. As projects were reaching their culmination, the COVID-19 pandemic closed schools and all participants had to abruptly pivot to virtual learning. This forced the group to go virtual as well. As a group, we took a step back from the projects—even as they lingered in various stages of completion—and became a support network for each other as we were thrust into the challenges posed by the pandemic. While we tried to continue our projects, we recognized that the radical change in circumstances made the projects as we had originally envisioned them impossible and that a new set of challenges was rapidly emerging.

Cohort 3

As Cohort 3 got underway in the fall of 2020, the education landscape remained uncertain, and many things were changing personally and professionally for the educators of *Teaching Out Loud*. We lost some members along the way due to a variety of factors and began the year with the original four members, Katy, Damon, Amanda, and Kahlil, and three of the added members from Cohort 2, Linnea, Kris, and Sarah. Due to the state of the world, we opted not to add any additional members to the group and to focus on creating shared spaces of support and working on coalescing our learning.

THE CIRCLE OF INQUIRY AND TEACHER RESEARCH AS RADICAL PRACTICE

In addition to having a strong foundation in critical literacy, the work of *Teaching Out Loud* is framed around practices of teacher research, including the circle of inquiry (Sinnema & Aitken, 2016). The circle of inquiry is a theoretical model that involves three processes: (1) raising questions, (2) collecting data/making sense of the data, and (3) taking action (Agency by Design, n.d.). These steps are cyclical and recursive, and thus fluidity exists in how educators move through the circle. This process works well for educators because they are responsible for the classroom space and act as participant-researchers as they enact inquiries in their classroom spaces (Lee, 2020). The first part of the process—raising questions—involves identifying tension, conflict, or dissonance that exists in the classroom space, examining why it exists, and reflecting on the "story of the question," or the event or moment that sparked the initial question. In the next stage—collecting data/making sense of the data—an educator collects a variety of data to help make sense of her or his specific question. Data could include notes from a lesson, the physical lesson plan, the products of teaching the lesson (slide decks, handouts, etc.), and/or student work (Ministry of Education, 2011). Once the data is collected, a teacher then begins the process of analysis or making sense of the data by considering how it informs practice. For the *Teaching Out Loud* educators, this analysis occurred individually and collectively. The final stage is taking action. Taking action is the summation of looking at practice and examining areas for change and growth and considering what new questions have formed as a result of the inquiry. Because classrooms are living and breathing entities, this is the process in theory, but there are a lot of factors at play and this, in turn, makes the actual process more complex, exciting, and uncertain (Aitken, n.d.).

Using the circle of inquiry as a primary component of our practice reflects our commitments to the theory and practice of teacher research. Teacher research merges theory and practice in ways that generate opportunity and advance equity for youth. Educators who engage in continuous inquiry processes tend to be more active professionally, more critical of policies and research applied unilaterally, and more deeply connected with other educators (Goswami & Stillman, 1987). Thus, teacher research is concerned with knowledge—what counts as knowledge, who owns it, and how it might be mobilized in the interest of fostering equity in schools. Cochran-Smith and Lytle (1999, p. 18) argue that "the larger goal [of teacher research] is to create classrooms and schools where rich learning opportunities increase students' life chances and alter the cultures of teaching by altering the relations of power in schools and universities." Building upon these understandings of inquiry, we assert that teachers are generators of knowledge and that this knowledge is fundamental to the shaping and reshaping of educational institutions (Campano, 2007; Cochran-Smith & Lytle, 1999). As teacher researchers who "theorize from the thick of things" (Simon & Campano, 2013, p. 22), we aim to construct counternarratives about both students and teachers (Carini, 2001; Gonzalez et al., 2005) in lieu of relying on deficit discourses (Comber & Kamler, 2004) that position both groups as deviant or failing. We view teacher research, then, as a radical practice designed to upend "business as usual in schools" (Cochran-Smith & Lytle, 2009) and imagine new possibilities for the future.

GROUP PRACTICES, NEW IDEAS OF PROFESSIONAL DEVELOPMENT, AND SOCIAL JUSTICE INQUIRY

As a collective, we created norms and practices that center teacher inquiry and reflection as educators. As a collective, we established a space that focused not only on the content of our meetings but on their processes as well. In cocreating processes that support and nurture our learning as educators, we aimed to create spaces that were counter to traditional professional development and that centered on social justice pedagogy. Building on philosophies that center student and educator voice, we developed a check-in process that allowed for deep sharing and became a central component of our monthly meetings. Over the lifespan of the group, we have used these check-ins at the start of each meeting. These have taken on a variety of formats, including story circles, a professional/personal highlight, a rose and a thorn, and open discussion. Beginning our sessions with these check-ins allows us as educators to reflect our shared humanity and acknowledge that we have intersectional complex social locations that extend beyond the one dimension of being educators.

Within the *Teaching Out Loud* community, we define traditional professional development as training that is implemented via the school or district that is used to fulfill requirements rather than promote educator growth. In contrast, we view *Teaching Out Loud* as a departure from traditional professional development spaces as it centers educators, focuses on teacher inquiry, and aims at creating opportunities for the real and sustained growth of all individuals involved in the process. We conceptualize this as part of a larger, complex, dynamic web of meaning-making, which was not available to participants in top-down professional development that is often used in school and district settings. Thus, we argue it is a space of radical professional development, social justice professional development, and a space that aims to combat the oppressive institution of traditional professional development.

The *Teaching Out Loud* space not only acts as a way to reinvent and recast what authentic professional development can and should be, it also allows each educator to redesign their classroom curriculum, their ideas of what education spaces can be, and the ways in which they view themselves (Anderson & Cohen, 2015). As a collective, the idea of "redesign" became central to the growth of each educator. The group space in itself was a redesign of traditional professional development, and the projects noted earlier are redesigns of ways to teach a variety of subjects and ideas, but through social justice lenses that invited students into learning in intentional, and often radical, ways. Thus, as this was central to the work overall, it influenced how we created the space and enacted our inquiry as individuals and as a *Teaching Out Loud* collective.

In addition to the personal monthly check-ins, we use a variety of other teacher inquiry practices that emphasize teachers' classroom knowledge. For example, each teacher regularly shares artifacts from her or his project and, using inquiry protocols, we collectively analyze these artifacts to evoke insights. The process usually works as follows: (1) the educator-researcher distributes data and provides necessary context, (2) the group takes time to individually examine the data, (3) educators then gather in a circle to offer insights and feedback on the data. The first round focuses solely on noticing (limited to concrete observations). In the second round, participants make connections to issues, concepts, books, research, etc. In the third round, participants raise questions, and in the fourth round offer suggestions or recommendations for moving forward. To end the session, the educator-researcher addresses the group with any responses to questions, clarifications, nascent insights, and so on. This analysis exercise requires vulnerability, as we must make the intimate aspects of our teaching practice visible to others. Artifacts that teachers choose to highlight vary. Some examples of items brought to the group include student work samples, teaching materials (lesson plans, slide sets, etc.), articles pertaining to the topic of the lesson, excerpts from texts used in the work, photos of the project, and more. Teachers consistently leave these data analysis sessions with rich perspectives on their practice and concrete ideas regarding how to move the work forward.

In addition to the group practices and processes documented earlier, *Teaching Out Loud* is also a formal research project; as such, we collect and analyze data about the group and publish it widely. For example, all *Teaching Out Loud* meetings were audio-recorded and transcribed. Katy, the group facilitator, also records field notes during every session and has conducted interviews with all participants at various points throughout the project. Educator-participants are also asked to complete final projects/reflective writing at the end of each academic year, which are not only important to the inquiry process but also become a source of data. These represent a variety of modalities, including formal written reports, slide presentations, letters, oral presentations, and artistic representations of the year. These reports/reflections are another source of data that aids in driving group decisions and the *Teaching Out Loud* work overall. Through these pieces, we can trace our work as individuals and groups through the years, and they aid in situating our data points in context with the larger world. Although Katy primarily took responsibility for collecting the data, analysis was done collaboratively as a group and often involved reading through data, identifying emerging themes, and triangulating themes across data sources. Having this data aided in both group development and noting structures and networks of inner support that we could each use that extended beyond the larger group. For example, Kahlil and Damon both noted that their work centered on a vulnerability that is often viewed negatively as male-identified educators from marginalized communities. Noting this connection afforded a deeper partnership between them as they consider how to combat endemic inequities in the education system through vulnerability. Thus, data analysis and collection occurred on two levels. Individuals collected data on and analyzed their own practice while the group worked together to analyze how *Teaching Out Loud* practices, processes, and inquiry approaches might be applicable to educators across divergent contexts.

SHARING AS RECENTERING EDUCATOR VOICE

A large component of *Teaching Out Loud* focuses on making our work public. This is multifold, as it allows for educators to understand new perspectives of how to use social justice pedagogy in their own spaces, show other educators and policymakers the critical nature of educational spaces, demonstrate how classrooms act as living labs that mirror the world around them, and lastly provide the educators with an opportunity to have their voices heard. Educator voice is often absent in our society as teachers continue to be devalued. For this reason, we have collectively worked to showcase the work of *Teaching Out Loud* via class presentations for preservice educators, conference presentations, articles, and other written works such as the volume you are currently reading. We work from a collective writing space where all educators have the opportunity to have their voice directly heard. Therefore, we aim to share our stories as educators in as many spaces as possible, and by sharing our stories we hope to inspire other educators to make their work public and demonstrate how they are creating and enacting spaces that allow students to become more aware of themselves, others, and the world around them.

TEACHING, LEARNING, AND GROWING IN CONTENTIOUS TIMES

The *Teaching Out Loud* fellowship was established to create and maintain authentic spaces for educator growth through humanizing and hyperlocalized professional development. What it means to be teaching, learning, and growing in contentious times has become even more of the reality as education and educational spaces have been politicized even further with the onset of the COVID-19 pandemic. Educators had to pivot to virtual learning overnight as the cracks in the system and the lack of equity were illuminated in stark and unexpected ways. While inequity has permeated American education since its inception, the pandemic has highlighted these inequities. This is the landscape that *Teaching Out Loud* works to combat as educators seek to teach, learn, and grow in the most contentious of times.

NOTES

1. *Hxstory* as opposed to *history* is used throughout as a means to disrupt the heteropatriarchy that is tied to the term history and its centering of the notion of power among cisgender male peoples.

2. Names of group members who do not have chapters in the book have been changed to protect their anonymity.

REFERENCES

Agency by Design. (n.d.). Designing and documenting: The inquiry cycle. Agency by Design. http://www.agencybydesign.org/inquiry-cycle

Aitken, G. (2018, June 8). How to undertake teaching as inquiry. The Education Hub. https://theeducationhub.org.nz/how-to-undertake-teaching-as-inquiry/

Anderson, G., & Cohen, M. I. (2015). Redesigning the identities of teachers and leaders: A framework for studying new professionalism and educator resistance. *Education Policy Analysis Archives*, *23*, 85.

Bartolome, L. I. (1994). Beyond the methods fetish: Toward a humanizing pedagogy. *Harvard Educational Review*, *64*(2), 173–194.

Campano, G. (2007). *Immigrant students and literacy: Reading, writing, and remembering*. Teachers College Press.

Carini, P. F. (2001). *Starting strong: A different look at children, schools, and standards.* Teachers College Press.

Cochran-Smith, M., & Lytle, S. (1999). Relationships of knowledge and practice: Teacher learning in communities. *Review of Research in Education, 24,* 249–305.

Cochran-Smith, M., & Lytle, S. (2009). *Inquiry as stance: Practitioner research for the next generation.* Teachers College Press.

Collins, P. H, & Bilge, S. (2016). *Intersectionality.* Polity Press.

Comber, B., & Kamler, B. (2004). Getting out of deficit: Pedagogies of reconnection. *Teaching Education, 15*(3), 293–310.

Crawford-Garrett, K., Sánchez, R. M., & Meyer, R. J. (2018). Problematizing silence, practicing dissent: Engaging preservice teachers in a critique of the current political times. *New Educator, (14)*1, 42–58.

Crenshaw, K. (1989). Demarginalizing the intersection of race and sex: A Black feminist critique of antidiscrimination doctrine, feminist theory and antiracist politics. *University of Chicago Legal Forum, 1989*(1), 139–167.

del Carmen Salazar, M. (2013). A humanizing pedagogy: Reinventing the principles and practice of education as a journey toward liberation. *Review of Research in Education, 37*(1), 121–148.

Fast, J. (2018). In defense of safe spaces: A phenomenological account. *Atlantis: Critical Studies in Gender, Culture & Social Justice / Études Critiques Sur Le Genre, La Culture, et La Justice, 39*(2), 1–22.

Freire, P. (2000). *Pedagogy of the oppressed.* Continuum.

González, N., Moll, L. C., & Amanti, C. (2005). *Funds of knowledge: Theorizing practice in households, communities, and classrooms.* L. Erlbaum Associates.

Goswami, D., & Stillman, P. (1987). *Reclaiming the classroom: Teacher research as an agency for change.* Boynton/Cook.

Gould, J. (2012). *Learning theory and classroom practice in the lifelong learning sector.* SAGE.

Huerta, T. M. (2011). Humanizing pedagogy: Beliefs and practices on the teaching of Latino children. *Bilingual Research Journal, 34*(1), 38–57.

Kelly, B. T., & Bhangal, N.K. (2018). Life Narratives as a pedagogy for cultivating critical self-reflection. *New Directions for Student Leadership, 159,* 41–52.

Lee, L. (2020, February 26). The benefits of inquiry-based PD. Edutopia. https://www.edutopia.org/article/benefits-inquiry-based-pd

Ministry of Education. (2011). Understanding teaching as inquiry. *New Zealand Curriculum Update, 12,* 1–4.

Simon, R., & Campano, G. (2013). Activist literacies: Teacher research as resistance to the "normal curve." *Journal of Language and Literacy Education, 9*(1), 21–39.

Sinnema, C., & Aitken, G. (2016). Teaching as inquiry. In Fraser, D. & Hill, M. (Eds.), *The professional practice of teaching in New Zealand* (pp. 79–97). Cengage Learning.

Stevenson, L. M., & Deasy, R. (2005). *Third space: When learning matters.* Arts Education Partnership.

CHAPTER 3

Educational Opportunities and Challenges in New Mexico

Katherine Crawford-Garrett, Damon R. Carbajal,
Amanda Y. Short, and Kahlil Simpson

INTRODUCTION

In 2018, Judge Sarah Singleton ruled that the state of New Mexico had failed to comply with state and federal laws regarding the education of Native American students, English language learners (ELLs), and students with disabilities (Walsh, 2021). The case, *Yazzie/Martinez v. State of New Mexico*, hinges upon the idea that the New Mexico Public Education Department (NMPED) has failed to provide a "uniform and sufficient" educational program for all students as outlined by Article XII, section 1 of the New Mexico Constitution (State of New Mexico, 2021). Stemming from the decision, the state is tasked with addressing a lack of funding in programs benefiting hxstorically marginalized students, the availability and quality of full-day pre-K, the recruitment of highly trained teachers, and a lack of funding and oversight within districts.

The decision has been deemed a landmark case (Muñiz, 2022) not only for its demands of collegiate readiness for all students but for the bringing to light a hxstory of systemic undermining of the educational success of hxstorically marginalized students.

The trial was widely viewed as a major success for the students and communities of New Mexico. Yet 2 years after the decision, despite frequent outcry from tribal leaders and the plaintiffs themselves (Leno and Martinez, 2021; McKay, 2021), the state has failed to operationalize the verdict in a manner that directly impacts students.

Building upon the *Yazzie/Martinez* lawsuit, our goal in this chapter is to situate the sociopolitical and hxstorical context of teaching and learning in New Mexico, recognizing that New Mexico presents a unique set of opportunities and challenges that are seldom acknowledged or understood in national education discourse. We frame our arguments within the concept of agency in order to consider the ways in which various New Mexico communities have fought for access to education within and against the devastating effects of colonialism, White supremacy, and English-only policies. We also document more recent efforts to curb teacher agency through the application of neoliberal, market-based initiatives and offer examples of teacher resistance. In doing so, we aim to generate a rich portrait of New Mexico and to illustrate how *Teaching Out Loud* was continually shaped and reshaped by this intricate interplay of forces. We begin with a very brief overview of the hxstory of education in New Mexico. Next, we conceptualize teacher agency by drawing on ecological perspectives. We then detail several recent policy interventions, including school grading and value-added models of teacher evaluation, and describe how these interventions have profoundly impacted teachers and schools. We end with a brief overview of the COVID-19 pandemic and its potential and pitfalls in redressing years of stark educational inequities in New Mexico.

HXSTORY AND BACKGROUND ON NEW MEXICO

New Mexico has been a site of social and political struggle since well before it became a U.S. state in 1912 (and one of the last to enter the union) (Gonzales, 2015). New Mexico is home to 23 distinct tribes, including 19 pueblo communities who have inhabited the land since time immemorial. Educational policies implemented in the wake of Spanish and settler colonization, specifically in the late 19th century (Martinez, 2021), had devastating effects on indigenous communities in New Mexico (and elsewhere) as children were stripped of language and culture through the process of forced assimilation (Reyhner & Eder, 2004). For example, boarding school initiatives, designed to "Americanize" indigenous youth, tore families apart as children were separated from parents and elders and required to conform to European customs and Western epistemologies (Chavéz, 1997). While boarding schools still exist in New Mexico—the Santa Fe Indian School being one example—they have been reclaimed as sites of cultural preservation and offer opportunities for Native youth to be educated according to indigenous worldviews (Hyer, 1990).

Mexican American youth faced similar challenges as children were punished for speaking Spanish and equal access to schools and opportunities was severely limited (Gokee et al., 2020). In some cases, Mexican American families used lawsuits and judicial processes to try and rectify existing disparities, specifically around language education (Powers, 2014). In addition, Mexican American youth have faced added obstacles in relation to access, not only with language but also persecution based on documentation status—sentiments that were heightened in the Trump administration but had existed long before (Goldsmith et al., 2018). Thus, New Mexican hxstory casts a long and complex shadow as the state must reconcile with the ways in which intergenerational trauma continues to impact communities (Sosa-Provencio et al., 2020).

New Mexico is often depicted negatively in public policy and media accounts, which focus on students' low levels of achievement on standardized measures, high rates of children living in poverty, poor nutrition, and excessive levels of drug and alcohol abuse (Contreras, 2020; Hagemeyer et al., 2018; NMPED, n.d.). In these media portrayals, little attention is dedicated to the hxstorical context mentioned earlier or to the intergenerational trauma that continues to impact hxstorically marginalized communities who have been subjected to abusive educational practices and policies. In the 2020 Chance-for-Success Index, which measures access to educational opportunities, New Mexico ranked last (Education Week, 2020). It also ranked at or near the bottom for parental education and parental employment. Moreover, in 2017, over 27% of adults in the state were living below the poverty line, one of the highest rates of poverty in the country (Ujifusa, 2020). In many ways, the COVID-19 pandemic only highlighted these disparities. Native communities across the state faced staggering case counts early on (Acosta et al., 2021) and were often contending with food insecurity and a lack of access to fresh water prior to COVID-19 (Sagaskie, 2019). Moreover, rural communities in New Mexico who lack Wi-Fi access encountered substantial obstacles during virtual schooling and struggled to provide students with the tools and resources necessary to keep learning continuous.

The challenges that surfaced during COVID-19 illustrated the profound legacies of federal and state policies that have lacked community voice or input and systematically undermined hxstorically marginalized communities. In 2011, Governor Susanna Martinez hired Hanna Skandera as state education secretary. Under Skandera the New Mexico educational system underwent an overhaul that aligned with techniques and approaches used by Jeb Bush's administration to reform education in Florida (McShane, 2018). Under the leadership of Martinez and Skandera, the state adopted two controversial approaches to improving schools: school grading (i.e., labeling schools on an A–F scale according to student performance on standardized tests) and value-added models of teacher evaluation (in which teachers are assessed, in part, on student growth on standardized tests) (Brown, 2015). It is difficult to overstate how deeply these policies impacted educators in New Mexico and how much they ultimately impeded teacher agency. To illustrate the role of state and federal policy interventions on teacher agency, we discuss the policy of "school grading" with particular attention to how this policy impacted educators in one school community and how educators actively resisted efforts to curb their autonomy. First, we theorize teacher agency according to ecological models and then we illustrate the way school grading impeded teacher agency in fundamental ways.

ECOLOGICAL CONCEPTIONS OF TEACHER AGENCY

The term agency is utilized frequently in educational literature, yet seldom adequately defined, resulting in reductive understandings that consistently equate agency with action. For the purposes of our analysis, we draw on ecological approaches to define teacher agency, acknowledging that agency can be understood phenomenologically and is both relational and temporal and thus extends beyond individual actions (Priestly et al., 2015, p. 20). In other words, agency emerges in particular contexts as the result of the interplay of a number of factors, including social relationships, past experiences, and future aspirations (p. 20). Moreover, we view agency as intimately tied to social justice efforts; even as real societal structures exist that have hxstorically contributed to the maintenance of oppressive structures, we recognize that teachers can and do make meaningful efforts to transform those structures in schools and classrooms. In fact, "one of the basic assumptions of teachers acting as agents of social justice is that they *believe* such agency is part of their professional role" (Pantic, 2017, p. 220). While neoliberal reform efforts consistently depict teachers as technicians and foreground compliance, critical educators seek to transcend this positioning through their beliefs and actions (Villegas & Lucas, 2002). Transformative power, then, is inherently connected to teachers' abilities to not only critically reflect upon their current conditions but also to imagine more empowering alternatives.

For the past 2 decades, researchers have documented the ways in which teachers have responded to the various metrics of control instituted as part of neoliberal reform efforts. For example, when teachers in California were forced to demonstrate "fidelity" to a prescribed reading curriculum, they strategically utilized relationships with university mentors and other educator networks to deliver instruction that felt responsive to the needs of students and aligned with their professional principles (Achinstein & Ogawa, 2006). Similarly, when teachers in a Los Angeles elementary school were faced with a hostile principal and a literacy curriculum that failed to build upon the children's cultural and linguistic assets, they cocreated alternative approaches to literacy instruction, connecting with key advocates outside of their school setting (Ryan, 2017). In yet another example, educators in the southwestern United States reappropriated policy texts meant to position them as failing and redesigned them as agentive documents that highlighted their criticality and expertise as educators (Crawford-Garrett, Perez & Short, 2016). Teachers in Philadelphia used professional book clubs to collectively problematize topics like school discipline, high-stakes accountability, and institutional racism, among others, as they imagined alternative possibilities for schools and classrooms (Riley & Cohen, 2018). These examples are closely aligned with ecological perspectives on agency as teachers strategically considered the complexity of school and classroom contexts, leveraged collegial relationships, built upon previous experiences with social justice activism, and foregrounded their hopes and goals for students in designing curricular and pedagogical experience

Enacting teacher agency through resistance is not only humanizing, it is central to the "literacies of teaching," which Lytle (2006) defines as "[engaging] in an ongoing, searching, and sometimes profoundly unsettling dialogue with students, families, administrators, policy makers, and other teachers who may talk, read and write from very different locations and experiences" (p. 259). As we talked openly as members of *Teaching Out Loud* across dimensions of difference that included age, race, social class, sexuality, teaching experience, ethnicity, and gender, we collectively pushed our teaching to more daring and more vulnerable spaces. By sharing readings, data, and experiences from our individual school sites, we came away changed, both as people and as political actors capable of shaping and re-shaping institutional contexts.

As other researchers have asserted (Pantic, 2017; Priestley et al., 2015), these kinds of relationships are central to teacher agency. In countless instances, teachers in the *Teaching Out Loud* fellowship program were emboldened by each other's stories, challenged to expand their repertoires, and encouraged to center criticality in their work. As neoliberalism increasingly encroaches upon all public sectors, maintaining human relationships that allow for intimacy and vulnerability is of paramount importance. As Lytle (2006) notes, there is a "pressing need to create collegial contexts for learning that reflect local culture, exist over time, foster enduring relationships and networks, and intentionally interrupt the taken-for-granted alliances of power/knowledge implicit and often explicit in much of the current policy discourse related to teaching and student performance" (p. 259). Further, *Teaching Out Loud* offered an intergenerational space where preservice and in-service teachers could share and theorize openly—albeit from different social locations—as they refined their teaching philosophies and considered what it means to teach in "these times" (Lytle, 2006).

SCHOOL GRADING

An apt example of the impact of school grading on local communities began 15 years ago at Nopal Elementary [pseudonym], where Amanda, Kris, and Linnea teach. At the time, Nopal had just over 500 students representing a wide range of New Mexican cultures and languages, including Pueblo,

Diné, Mexican, Latinx, Hispanic, White, and Asian. The school also included a wide range of socioeconomic backgrounds from students who were intermittently homeless to those from solidly middle-class families. As the education landscape in New Mexico shifted, so did the demographics and curricular priorities of Nopal Elementary. For example, Nopal was known throughout the city for its Spanish dual-language program as well as support programs for Native American students run by Native American educators. Fifteen years ago, teachers created and developed curriculum to fit students' needs with support from their colleagues. The district provided math, science, and literacy curriculum, but it was largely viewed as a resource rather than a mandate, as were a variety of other curricula and professional development (PD) opportunities offered by the district.

Then, corporate reform began to trickle down to Nopal. The first noticeable change was the implementation of the Baldrige Framework of plan-do-study-act (Ruben & Gigliotti, 2019). This framework originated in corporate America, and the school district invested significant tax dollars in requiring teachers to implement the framework in their classrooms. Teachers at Nopal Elementary began posting *plan-do-study-act* bulletin boards in their classrooms that included graphs and charts of student progress. They spent time creating *plans for progress*, implementing these plans, interpreting data related to the plans, and *acting* on that data. To many of the teachers at Nopal, this was busy work, dumbing down the more important dimensions of their classroom curriculum. For example, prior to Baldridge, teachers were already setting goals for their students based on student need and state standards and then collecting meaningful data to monitor progress toward these goals. With Baldridge, the principal and the district came to check to see if teachers had *proof of progress* displayed in their rooms. For many educators, this heavy-handed oversight indexed the beginning of doing meaningless paperwork to "prove" that teachers were teaching. The classroom climate began to shift as teachers focused more on collecting data points instead of holistic learning. Students began to spend time graphing their progress and copying personal goals into data binders rather than exploring and investigating. Everyone was focusing on showing progress with graphs and charts and less on showing progress through portfolios and performance assessments. The classroom soon felt more like a cookie-cutter factory and less like an individualized learning environment.

Then, as more time progressed, the requirements from outside grew exponentially. The computer programs *SuccessMaker* (SuccessMaker, 2022) and *Waterford* (Waterford, 2022) became required for "struggling" students. Ultimately, New Mexico adopted a controversial school grading system (New Mexico Public Education Department, n.d.) and value-added models for teacher evaluations, hallmarks of the neoliberal turn in school reform. When the grading system first appeared, Nopal was labeled with an F. The principal at the time tried to explain away this grade to affluent parents by noting the school's high population of students in special education. Because the school grade was (supposedly) tied to high-stakes testing (the formula was not made clear to anyone), what followed was a flurry of changes in curriculum. A portion of the day was dedicated to practicing writing short answers for the test, and students studied test-specific vocabulary. Then the curriculum requirements began to change. Teachers were given a math and literacy curriculum that would prepare students for the test. Instead of reading books for enjoyment from our school bookroom and participating in book discussions and literary debate or relevant vocabulary development, students were required to annotate the text in a textbook reader and respond to short-answer recall questions. Not only were student responses limited to recall, but the texts were Eurocentric and East Coast American (i.e., stories referenced basements and attics—things fairly uncommon to students in the Southwest). Along with this, more short-cycle assessments that closely aligned to the high-stakes testing and helped better "prepare" students became required. In addition, teachers were given a gag order through state legislation about testing—they could not "disparage" the test. This meant that if a parent asked about the high-stakes test, a teacher could not offer an honest opinion about it.

A group of teachers from Nopal began to fight back. They held meetings with parents after school hours in order to explain the damage constant testing caused to the education system. They discussed trends of the grading system: schools in primarily White neighborhoods received higher grades than those in Black and Brown neighborhoods. Teachers stuck together and refused to do busy work required by the state (i.e., bubbling test answers on a scantron sheet) and spoke out about their poor evaluations to parents, the media, and the school board, burning them publicly at the school board offices in 2015 (Bush, 2015; Hooks, 2015). A group of teachers and a parent from Nopal Elementary worked with the American Civil Liberties Union (ACLU) to sue the public education department in order to change the regulations preventing teachers from speaking out against the testing (McCoy, 2016). They won the lawsuit, allowing teachers to speak freely about the testing and the damages it causes to children.

But as the F label on Nopal Elementary and its community stuck, the population at the school slowly began to change. Affluent, White families within walking distance of the school began to take their students to charter schools or private schools or other public schools that didn't have the stigma of the "F" label (New Mexico Senate Democrats, 2014). The majority of the school's population became more and more impoverished as many faced food insecurity and lived precarious lives in low-rent hotels or subsisted on government vouchers. As this portion of the population grew, so did the percentage of students who experienced intergenerational trauma caused by the cycle of poverty (Johnson, 2020; Linthicum, 2018). And so, the cycle continued. As Nopal's population became needier, test scores continued to fall, affluent families continued to move away, and stricter curricular mandates that dominated the school day were instituted. The final result: Nopal works hard to support high-needs students with very limited resources.

THE COVID-19 PANDEMIC AND NEW MEXICO EDUCATION

Beginning in March 2020, New Mexico schools, like almost all schools across the United States and the world, were shut down, and panic emerged as virtual learning ensued. As teachers and students grappled with this transition, often feeling isolated, overwhelmed, and woefully unprepared, the cracks that run deep in our nation and go all the way to the core of our existence (Sosa-Provencio et al., 2020) were revealed. The wealth gap of students and educators was shown drastically via the lack or inclusion of resources, such as stable Internet, reliable computers, and space to work in. This wealth gap is one that we need to examine from a social justice and intersectional perspective. If we examine school demographics (both from a student and educator point of view), we note that there is a lot of variation in schools across New Mexico, but this is not considered when a one-size-fits-all approach is used. This illuminates the ways in which education is entrenched in White supremacy and how privilege plays into the political landscape of schooling, leaving many to fend for themselves (Allen et al., 2019). Those who had access to technology and the Internet were able to make a more seamless transition to the virtual world, but those who were without were left to struggle. We must also acknowledge the gatekeeping that occurs daily with the education system, whether that be with technology, funds, or any other facet that goes into creating and maintaining schooling spaces.

The rural/frontier spaces in New Mexico that are inhabited by many Black, Indigenous, People of Color (BIPOC) students—specifically Native American and Mexicana/o/x—had few resources available to them to support pandemic learning (Silva, 2022). This is illuminated by the lack of both technology and Internet access in rural spaces across the state (New Mexico Center on Law and Poverty, 2020). Thus, COVID-19 has shone a light on how years of neglect and underresourcing has contributed to a highly inequitable educational system.

As the pandemic further politicized education in New Mexico and politicians debated vaccination policies, masking, and in-person versus virtual learning, the experiences, perspectives, and concerns of educators and students were seldom included in state-level decision-making processes.

These political tensions are further heightened by legislation like "Don't Say Gay" bills (Pendharkar, 2022) as well as the ongoing battle over the role of critical race theory in K–12 schools (Lepore, 2022). In other words, the tensions New Mexico experienced during the COVID-19 pandemic reflect the sociopolitical and hxstorical complexities of the state in which disparities are endemic, rooted in racist and colonial practices, and continue into today. As long as our educational system is driven by the interplay of money, power, privilege, and politics, fundamental shifts in favor of equity and diversity are unlikely to occur. Instead, educators and students will need to enact change at local levels by advancing teacher agency as large-scale change remains elusive.

CONCLUSION

The impact of neoliberal reforms on schools and classrooms across the globe has been profound. New Mexico has been no exception. Contending with the lingering effects of colonialism, English-only practices, and White supremacist policies enacted over centuries, New Mexico needs a transformational vision for education that truly centers on students and communities. Moreover, teachers committed to teaching differently and teaching responsively must find new ways to advance agency as they take bold steps to reclaim their profession within and against contexts that continually depict them as technicians tasked with compliance. Ecological perspectives on agency offer empowering alternatives for teachers who are seeking ways to utilize agency in the interest of fostering equity across the P–20 spectrum. By drawing upon past experiences, leveraging networks and relationships—including inquiry communities—and contextualizing present practices within and against future aspirations, teachers have the potential to transform schools and classrooms and promote lasting institutional change.

REFERENCES

Achinstein, B., & Ogawa, R. (2006). (In)Fidelity: What the resistance of new teachers reveals about professional principles and prescriptive educational policies. *Harvard Educational Review, 76*(1), 30–63.

Acosta, A. M., Garg, S., Pham, H., Whitaker, M., Anglin, O., O'Halloran, A., Milucky, J., Patel, K., Taylor, C., Wortham, J., Chai, S. J., Kirley, P. D., Alden, N. B., Kawasaki, B., Meek, J., Yousey-Hindes, K., Anderson, E. J., Openo, K. P.,

Weigel, A., Monroe, M. L., Ryan, P., Reeg, L., Kohrman, A., Lynfield, R., Bye, E., Torres, S., Salazar-Sanchez, Y., Muse, A., Barney, G., Bennet, N. M., Bushey, S., Billing, L., Shiltz, E., Sutton, M., Abdullah, N., Talbot, K., Schaffner, W., Ortega, J., Price, A., Fry, A. M., Hall, A., Kim, L., & Havers, F. P. (2021). Racial and ethnic disparities in rates of COVID-19-associated hospitalization, intensive care unit admission, and in-hospital death in the United States from March 2020 to February 2021. *JAMA Network Open, 4*(10), 1–15.

Allen, R. L., Liou, D. D., Welton, A., Diem, S., & Carpenter, B. W. (2019). Managing whiteness: The call for educational leadership to breach the contractual expectations of White supremacy. *Urban Education, 54*(5), 677–705.

Brown, E. (2015, November 12). Education researchers caution against using students' test scores to evaluate teachers. *The Washington Post.* https://www.washingtonpost.com/local/education/education-researchers-caution-against-using-value-added-models—ie-test-scores—to-evaluate-teachers/2015/11/12/72b6b45c-8950-11e5-be39-0034bb576eee_story.html

Bush, M. (2015, May 2). APS teachers burn their evaluations in protest. *The Albuquerque Journal.* https://www.abqjournal.com/587949/aps-teachers-burn-their-evals.html

Chavéz, C. R. (1997). Book review-Education for extinction: American Indian and the boarding school experience, 1875–1928. *New Mexico Historical Review, 72*(2), 197–198.

Contreras, R. (2020, January 15). New Mexico child poverty ranking back to 49th in nation, Kids Count report finds. New Mexico Voices for Children. https://www.nmvoices.org/archives/13830

Crawford-Garrett, K., Perez, M., & Short, A. (2016). Leveraging literacies for social change: Portraits of teacher resistance at an "F" school. *Teaching Education, 28*(3), 227–243.

Education Week. (2020, January 21). State grades on chance for success: 2020 map and rankings. *Education Week.* https://www.edweek.org/policy-politics/state-grades-on-chance-for-success-2020-map-and-rankings/2020/01

Gokee, C., Stewart, H., & De Leon, J. (2020). Scales of suffering in the US-Mexico borderlands. *International Journal of Historical Archaeology, 24*(4), 823–851.

Goldsmith, P. R., Flores-Yeffal, N. Y., Salinas, J., Reese, B., & Cruz, C. E. (2018). Mexican parents' undocumented status and the educational attainment of the children left behind. *Social Science Research, 72*, 194–206.

Gonzales, P. B. (2015). New Mexico statehood and political inequality: The case of Nuevomexicanos. *New Mexico Historical Review, 90*(1), 31–52.

Hagemeyer, A., Azofeifa, A., Stroup, D. F., & Tomedi, L. E. (2018). Evaluating surveillance for excessive alcohol use in New Mexico. *Preventing Chronic Disease, 15.*

Hooks, C. (2015, May 21). Teachers protest, burn state-mandated evaluations. Taos News. https://www.taosnews.com/news/teachers-protest-burn-state-mandated-evaluations/article_2102c8ea-a8fa-55d7-b154-859fc38b1b49.html

Hyer, S. (1990). *One house, one voice, one heart: Native American education at the Santa Fe Indian School.* Museum of New Mexico Press.

Johnson, S. (2020, February 27). Breaking the cycle: Healing intergenerational trauma. *Santa Fe New Mexican*. https://www.santafenewmexican.com/life/teen/breaking -the-cycle-healing-intergenerational-trauma/article_888a2c60-572c-11ea-b991 -f307042dd039.html#:~:text=Loggains%20said%20New%20Mexico %20especially,education%20quality%20in%20the%20country

Leno, M., & Martinez J. (2021, September 5). 3 years after ruling, kids deserve first-rate education. *The Albuquerque Journal*. https://www.abqjournal.com /2426063/letters-218.html

Lepore, J. (2022, March 14). Why the school wars still rage. *The New Yorker*. https:// www.newyorker.com/magazine/2022/03/21/why-the-school-wars-still-rage

Linthicum, L. (2018, January 21). Kids in jeopardy a lasting crisis. *The Albuquerque Journal*. https://www.abqjournal.com/1122274/kids-in-jeopardy-a-lasting -crisis.html

Lytle, S. L. (2006). The literacies of teaching urban adolescents in these times. In D. Alvermann (ed.), *Reconceptualizing the Literacies in Adolescents' Lives*. (2nd ed.). Lawrence Erlbaum.

Martinez, R. (2021, June 4). Education in New Mexico has long, tenuous history. *Santa Fe New Mexican*. https://www.santafenewmexican.com/news/local_news /education-in-new-mexico-has-long-tenuous-history/article_f9621b04-c3ec -11eb-b8cd-9f0bfdb1bc48.html

McCoy, M. (2016, March 3). ACLU files speech lawsuit against New Mexico Public Education Department. ACLU New Mexico. https://www.aclu-nm.org/en /news/aclu-files-free-speech-lawsuit-against-new-mexico-public-education -department

McKay, D. (2021, July 3). Native leader blasts NM's response to education lawsuit. *The Albuquerque Journal*. https://www.abqjournal.com/2412541/native -leader-blasts-nms-response-to-education-lawsuit.html

McShane, M. Q. (2018, February 21). The New Mexico reform story. Education Next. https://www.educationnext.org/new-mexico-reform-story-hanna-skandera -legacy/

Muñiz, S. (2022, January 24). Community groups asking for state to update standards based on Yazzie/Martinez ruling. KOAT. https://www.koat.com/article /new-mexico-education-lawsuit-yazzie-martinez/38874521#

New Mexico Center on Law and Poverty. (2020, December 15). Yazzie plaintiffs ask court to order state to provide students computers and internet access. New Center on Law and Poverty. https://mailchi.mp/e52647a94998/yazzie -plaintiffs-ask-court-to-order-state-to-provide-students-computers-and-internet -access?e=d96b9b8193

New Mexico Public Education Department (NMPED). (n.d.). New Mexico: Academic performance. New Mexico Schools. https://newmexicoschools.com/state /999999/student-performance

New Mexico Senate Democrats. (2014, February 4). New Mexico educator and parent talk about state's education challenges. KRWG. https://www.krwg.org /local-viewpoints/2014-02-04/new-mexico-educator-and-parent-talk-about -states-education-challenges

Pantic, N. (2017). An exploratory study of teacher agency for social justice. *Teaching and Teacher Education, 66*, 219–231.

Pendhakar, E. (2022, March 18). Here's what Florida's 'don't say gay' and anti-'woke' bills actually say. *Education Week*. https://www.edweek.org/leadership/heres-what-floridas-dont-say-gay-and-anti-woke-bills-actually-say/2022/03?s_kwcid=AL!6416!3!486544088589!!!g!!&utm_source=goog&utm_medium=cpc&utm_campaign=ew+dynamic+recent%20&ccid=dynamic+ads+recent+articles&ccag=recent+articles+dynamic&cckw=&cccv=dynamic+ad&gclid=CjwKCAjwu_mSBhAYEiwA5BBmf4vn_QKoZGOpJ47XFkt7VHTqjMlftsAjmRo4upxrgvgvYfZinj7NrxoCuI4QAvD_BwE

Powers, J. M. (2014). From segregation to school finance: The legal context for language rights in the United States. *Review of Research in Education, 38*(1), 81–105.

Priestley, M., Biesta, G. J. J., & Robinson, S. (2015). *Teacher agency: An ecological approach*. Bloomsbury.

Reyhner, J. A., & Eder, J. M. O. (2004). *American Indian education: A history*. University of Oklahoma Press.

Riley, K. & Cohen, S. (Spring 2018). In Philadelphia, teacher book groups are the engines of change. *Rethinking Schools*, https://rethinkingschools.org/articles/in-philadelphia-teacher-book-groups-are-the-engines-of-change/

Ruben, B. D., & Gigliotti, R. A. (2019). The excellence in higher education model: A Baldrige-based tool for organizational assessment and improvement for colleges and universities. *Global Business & Organizational Excellence, 38*(4), 26–37.

Ryan, H. (2017). *Educational justice: Teaching and organizing against the corporate juggernaut*. Monthly Review Press.

Sagaskie, H. F. (2019). The impact of colonization: Food insecurity among American Indian and Alaskan Native adults. *Michigan Sociological Review, 33*, 101–114.

Silva, C. L. (2022, February 26). New Mexico students continue to learn remotely almost two years into the pandemic. Carlsbad Current Argus. https://www.currentargus.com/story/news/education/2022/02/26/why-some-new-mexico-students-continue-going-school-remotely/6668426001/

Sosa-Provencio, M. A., Sheahan, A., Desai, S., & Secatero, S. (2020). Tenets of "body-soul rooted pedagogy": Teaching for critical consciousness, nourished resistance, and healing. *Critical Studies in Education, 61*(3), 345–362.

State of New Mexico. (2021). New Mexico State Constitution. State of New Mexico. https://realfileee3072ab0d43456cb15a51f7d82c77a2.s3.amazonaws.com/e9efe992-dc26-4e1c-9560-53e5d77ded4d?AWSAccessKeyId=AKIAJBKPT2UF7EZ6B7YA&Expires=1654635597&Signature=%2BLbGStJXcS749O%2Bk6LEy939qrlU%3D&response-content-disposition=inline%3B%20filename%3D%22NM%20Constitution%202021%20SOS.pdf%22&response-content-type=application%2Fpdf

SuccessMaker. (2022, June 1). About us. SuccessMaker. https://www.savvas.com/index.cfm?locator=PS3d1m

Ujifusa, A. (2020, January 21). When it comes to nurturing student success, N.M. ranks last. Can it turn things around? *Education Week*. https://www.edweek.org/leadership/when-it-comes-to-nurturing-student-success-n-m-ranks-last-can-it-turn-things-around/2020/01

Villegas, A. M., & Lucas, T. (2002). Preparing culturally responsive teachers: Re-thinking the curriculum. *Journal of Teacher Education, 53*(1), 20–32.

Walsh, T. (2021, December 19). Lawmakers must tackle injustices to Native Americans. *The Albuquerque Journal.* https://www.abqjournal.com/2455082 /lawmakers-must-tackle-injustices-to-native-americans.html

Waterford. (2022, June 1). About Waterford.org. https://www.waterford.org/about/

TRANSLATING CRITICAL, CREATIVE WORK TO VIRTUAL SPACES: STORIES FROM THE CLASSROOM

CHAPTER 4

Promoting and Documenting the Importance of Play in a Kindergarten Classroom

Linnea Holden

ON REPEAT: A NOT-SO-NEW BEGINNING

It was 2018 and year 10 of my teaching career with Albuquerque Public Schools (APS) when yet another perfect storm of student trauma collided with a lack of specialized support for my kindergarten students. I had just returned to education after a much-needed 3-year hiatus. With shaky legs and renewed vigor, I had no idea that I was about to embark on my most challenging teaching years yet. Later, I will detail the deluge of difficulties that contributed to the 2018–2020 school years being pivotal for my growth as a teacher. It was a storm that had been brewing for the entirety of my career. I found that I could no longer teach in the service to standards, scripted curricula, and tests that did not reflect the reality of the human beings who were right in front of me each day. Children who yearned for control and ownership over some aspect of their lives. These kids needed time and space to play, explore, and socialize as they embarked on their careers in the public school system. I soon connected with the *Teaching Out Loud* inquiry group, where I began to reflect on and question the many years of district programs and mandates that had led me to neglect the purposeful integration of play in my teaching. I couldn't help but wonder, in the absence of ready access to district and school supports for the wide array of student needs in my classroom, how could I bring play back into the kindergarten classroom in an attempt to better support the whole child?

FINDING PRIORITIES

In addition to my 10 years as an elementary school teacher in New Mexico's largest city, I attended what were regarded as some of Albuquerque's toughest public schools. As a student, I benefited from my positionality as a White and Hispanic, northern New Mexican presenting as fully White with my red hair and freckles. I was also born into a working-class traditional family unit who was always able to make ends meet and then some. My upbringing took place in a rich variety of environments that included traditional New Mexican family gatherings centered around food and culture. This part of me intersected with the dominant White culture that was also a huge part of my identity and ethnicity. For the most part, I easily floated between worlds both socially and culturally. This was a privilege in so many ways. It allowed me to find and embrace my love of all things New Mexico. This is my place; these are my people.

Despite the real and persistent challenges associated with income inequality, I felt as though New Mexico could not be defined by its chronically higher-than-average poverty rate (Contreras, 2020). Instead, I saw beauty in the diversity and tenacity of the people and their valuable contributions to what it means to be New Mexican. As a high school and college student, I discovered my passion for working with children of all backgrounds. As an after-school program coordinator, a New Mexico Jazz Summer Camp counselor, a nanny, and a child-care worker, I witnessed joyful learning in the most playful of circumstances. It was apparent that children were electrified when given opportunities to make noise, make messes, and genuinely explore their surroundings.

These early experiences influenced my desire to grow my own capacity to teach through play and exploration. Sadly, I found that the reality of public education in the early and mid-2000s left little time for this. The priority during much of my teaching career was rooted in No Child Left Behind (NCLB) mandates that mostly included "rigorous" academic standards, excessive testing, scripted curricula, and harmful school grading practices (Gay, 2007).

When working toward my National Board Certification in 2014, I first dabbled in the art of going rogue. I learned that I could and should free myself from the constraints and limitations of a system that was undermining everything I knew and everything I wanted to learn about serving my students. Expensive curricula and restrictive district mandates did not help me identify or meet the needs of my students. With each year of my relatively short career, it became more and more undeniable that bucking the system was the only way. In achieving her National Board Certification, Gonzales (2013) describes the following: "Even if I have an unsupportive administration, toxic co-workers, limited supplies, it's on me. If the air conditioning goes out, if the Internet is down, it's on me to improvise, to model good character, to lead. Throw bad policy at me—I'll find a way to teach my students anyway. I know what I need to do. *I* am the teacher. *I* am the professional. It's on me" (para. 2).

My work in achieving National Board Certification marked the beginning of the end as I began to seriously question the status quo. It was also at this time that I took a 3-year break from teaching.

RETURN TO REALITY: A DELUGE OF CHALLENGES

Upon my return to APS in 2018, I found myself back in the kindergarten classroom with a full roster fluctuating at the high end of 20+ students and a revolving door of children moving in and out of our school boundaries each month. Along with the high rate of transiency, many of my students displayed a plethora of challenging behaviors that impacted the stability, well-being, and learning of every student in the classroom. On the more extreme end, one student struggled with long-lasting effects of in utero drug exposure, another was experiencing symptoms of a yet to be diagnosed mental illness, while still another was dubbed by his parents as "on the spectrum" but had not yet been officially identified by a professional or otherwise received any type of specialized support.

Each of these children could be aggressive, explosive, and destructive to peers, me, and the classroom environment. This included large and small objects being thrown; my students and myself being pushed, hit, and spit on; and curse words and obscenities directed at peers and teachers. Within those extremes, there were several students undergoing economic and familial struggles of all kinds. These children might come to school tired, hungry, depressed, or generally checked out. On any given day, I could expect small disagreements between peers, a cranky underslept child, and a traumatic event having occurred in a child's home life to set off a cascade of aggressive, disruptive, and generally chaotic incidents throughout the school day. Each day I went home emotionally and, at times, physically battered. I felt like a failure. I was not teaching content, I was struggling to manage a safe classroom, and I could barely keep up with the documentation needed to begin the very long referral process for my neediest students.

I wasn't alone. At union meetings, on public forums, and elsewhere, kindergarten teachers from around the district echoed these concerns. APS was seeing a new level of intensifying socioeconomic need that translated into acute negative behavioral and social-emotional demands within the regular education classroom. Far too many of Albuquerque's 4- and 5-year-olds were entering the public school system without having had access to early identification and interventions, quality prekindergarten, or parents armed with information on how to recognize and support the "normal" range of developmental and social-emotional milestones for young children.

SUPPORTING KINDERGARTEN THROUGH COLLABORATION, INQUIRY, AND REFLECTION

During my tumultuous return to teaching, I talked a lot with my good friend and colleague, Amanda. Amanda was witness to several tearful break-downs, during which she encouraged me to scale back on my academic goals for this class and explore alternative approaches, given the needs of my students. It was a long time coming in 2019, when I resolved to let go of the curriculum in order to explore a different approach to teaching in the name of child well-being. Almost simultaneously, Amanda invited me to participate in the teacher inquiry group, *Teaching Out Loud*. The timing could not have been more perfect. *Teaching Out Loud* became a welcoming, inspiring, and therapeutic teacher community for me. We were of all variet-ies who spent time learning about, reflecting on, and inquiring into teaching methods that would promote equity within our respective classrooms and education at large.

Monthly *Teaching Out Loud* meetings were a safe space to share, reflect, and develop personally and professionally. Each member's per-sonal and professional anecdotes fed connection and comradery as we got glimpses into one another's lives. While fellow member, Kahlil, taught middle school language arts, he and I both lamented the lack of support provided to students and families undergoing milestone school transitions. Kahlil saw the need to support 5th-graders as they transitioned to the novel demands of middle school routines and expectations. Similarly, it was ob-vious that many young children and families were undergoing a learning curve regarding the protocols and expectations related to the kindergarten classroom, school site, and the larger public school system (a transition that Kahlil's own son would undergo during our time collaborating in *Teaching Out Loud*). Damon, another *Teaching Out Loud* member, shared his work on educator mental health and self-care that was incredibly relevant as I continued to experience exhaustion and frustration. He consistently ac-knowledged the struggles of educators of all backgrounds and identities as he shared research and tested responsive practices to the harsh reality of teacher burnout.

It was during those early *Teaching Out Loud* meetings where I found space and support to develop my play-based inquiry goal in response to the kindergarten storm from the previous year and the equally challenging circumstances of my 2019–2020 students. Like the previous school year, each day could be wrought with classroom disruption and negative out-bursts of all kinds. The work of fellow *Teaching Out Loud* member, Sarah, underscored the need for me to change something in my approach to teach-ing young children. Sarah presented a video about the wide-ranging and long-lasting negative impacts of adverse childhood experiences (ACEs) on health and well-being. Sarah's sharing gave language and weight to what I was witnessing in the kindergarten classroom: children struggling with abuse, neglect, and household challenges that were wreaking havoc on their current health and well-being and could, no doubt, have long-term negative impacts on their lives (Felitti et al.,1998).

Additionally, due to NCLB's focus on test-measured, student academic achievement over all else, I found the kindergarten classroom still suffering the loss of play-based learning (Repko-Erwin, 2017). The social development, vocabulary, problem-solving, and critical thinking of students in Title 1 schools like mine have been especially negatively impacted due to their backgrounds of poverty. Allee-Herndon et al. (2021) identified play as a developmentally responsive practice that addresses equity issues experienced by more vulnerable students. My students were suffering in countless ways while my attention had been overly focused on standards and curriculum . . . again, the perfect storm for a dysfunctional early childhood learning environment. Yogman et al. (2018) found that "when play and safe, stable, nurturing relationships are missing in a child's life, toxic stress can disrupt the development of executive function and the learning of prosocial behavior; in the presence of childhood adversity, play becomes even more important" (para. 3). Because so many of my students were in precariously vulnerable and stressful situations, I decided to focus on increasing play in the classroom with the goal of providing an environment for my students to work on their pressing developmental and social-emotional needs.

GETTING STARTED: PRIORITIZING PLAYTIME

As I thought about my inquiry project, my excitement grew. I imagined the ways my inquiry project might support my students' development of self-regulation and social-emotional skills, and therefore, improve the overall learning environment. Mickleson (2019) states, "The level of academic expectations and the lack of time spent focusing on social development has led to a higher incidence of negative student behavior in the kindergarten classroom" (p. 65), a phenomenon that I was all too familiar with. To reverse this trend in my classroom, I first set off to rework my daily schedule to include time for play-integrated learning goals as well as unstructured self-selected play. This play-oriented schedule change was not completely revelatory to me, but I knew that I needed to explicitly prioritize it. I tended to look at the work being accomplished in the classrooms of my peers and feel as though, by not focusing more on structured and predetermined learning opportunities, I was neglecting kindergarten standards.

Furthermore, my administrator and I were still getting to know one another. Thus far, my experiences with him and anecdotes from my colleagues led me to believe that he trusted his staff and championed innovation. When reflecting with him on the intense behaviors exhibited by my students from the previous school year as well as those of the current year, I seized the moment to mention that I would be trying a new approach. I justified my position by discussing the social and emotional needs of my students. He reminded me that kindergarten was still an academic endeavor, not just a social-emotional one. While his comment made me nervous, he did not explicitly negate the idea.

Despite my determination to proceed with my project, it was a constant struggle for me to continuously refocus on my goal to center play and not get distracted by what looked like more academic progress in the classrooms of my colleagues. Additionally, I continued to wonder if my administration was right, that I might not be focusing enough on academics after all. I talked often with my *Teaching Out Loud* comrades about this tension. During one of our meetings, when asked to share about my inquiry project, I mentioned the anxiety that integrating play was creating for me: "One thing that I think the teacher has to let go of is the idea that your learning environment might look really unstructured and messy. To you and to an outsider." My comment was indicative of what I was telling myself on a daily basis in order to coach myself to keep going. It was obvious that I was undergoing a shift in thinking, stating, "You have to give the kids time and space to show their understanding of the materials and it's a lot of work." *Teaching Out Loud* was my sounding board while I reflected out loud to solidify my thoughts in a supportive environment.

With time to play articulated in my daily classroom schedule, I focused on finding ways to integrate it into targeted, academic learning goals. This is where I met a hurdle: limited play materials. While my classroom was stocked with a few traditional open-ended play items (wooden blocks, plastic manipulatives, a small kitchen set), there was limited variety, and many items were broken and ready to be retired. Additionally, having lightly explored Montessori methods, I had been inspired by the notion of simplifying the learning environment. Smith (2018) asserts that "when you tuck away 30%–50% of most children's toys (in a closet, garage, or other storage system), you may find they actually become more interested in what is on their shelves. This leads to longer periods of concentration, easier cleanup, greater independence . . ." (p. 60).

To increase toy rotation options, I had already begun searching thrift stores for viable play items. Then, I joyfully learned that each member of the *Teaching Out Loud* group was allotted $200 to support our respective inquiry projects.

Initially, I felt that simply "buying toys" might be a misuse of this funding. It felt frivolous, unnecessary, and even selfish when I knew the teachers in neighboring classrooms had similar shortages of quality play materials. I shared these doubts with *Teaching Out Loud* and considered creating a toy check-out library for the entire grade level to assuage my guilt. Talking with the group helped me realize that I did not have the time or energy to create a shared toy library: "And then, I thought, no, my own classroom needs better materials. Especially if I'm trying to teach certain concepts and I don't always have the play or open-ended tools and materials for the kids to go back and play within that concept . . . ." I could easily share with my peers without having to find time and space to organize such a structured scenario.

Next hurdle: What to buy? I began to develop standards for what I was looking for. The items needed to be novel and exciting, allow for open-ended exploration, and be sturdy enough to withstand the rigorous play of 5-year-olds. Smith (2018) encourages choosing "toys that will engage rather than entertain" (p. 60). In other words, I was looking for items that elicit active attention and creativity. There was so much out there! Magnetic building blocks (see Figure 4.2), manipulatives that suctioned and connected to one another, items that could serve to illustrate concepts of force and motion or simply allow students to explore sorting, building, sharing, and imagination. I presented the items I was considering purchasing to *Teaching Out Loud*. My voice must have still conveyed hesitancy. My colleagues encouraged me to take the plunge and make the purchases, reassuring me that these items were not just "toys" but would be important fuel for my inquiry project.

WHAT HAPPENS WHEN YOU LET THEM PLAY?

As play materials arrived, I experimented with how to introduce them into the learning environment. One example of my trial and error occurred when I presented colorfully patterned small amphibian and reptile manipulatives to support a math lesson plan that addressed counting with one-to-one correspondence. Once in their hands, children were keener to inspect, talk about, sort, and play with the items than to perform the very specific task that I had envisioned. I used the moment to let go of the assigned task and realized they needed time to explore these novel items. After a while, I attempted to direct their attention back towards the counting task. For example, "Anna,[1] I noticed you sorted the frogs from the lizards. I wonder how many each group has? Are there more frogs or lizards?" Sometimes a student would take my suggestion and begin counting and comparing. Other times, they would allow me to count to them or with them. Often, there was no interest in my guidance, so I receded into observation while they kept playing. Griffiths (1994) asserts the following regarding math play:

> Maths and play are very useful partners. If we want children to become successful mathematicians, we need to demonstrate to them that maths is enjoyable and useful, and that it can be a sociable and cooperative activity, as well as a quiet and individual one. We must be careful, too, to remember that play is not just a way of introducing simple ideas. Children will often set themselves much more difficult challenges if we give them control of their learning than if it is left up to the adults. (As cited in Özdoğan, 2011, p. 3119)

I experienced many of these moments where I grappled with my pursuit of predetermined learning goals versus allowing open exploration and learner agency. Another example occurred when I noticed José engaging his imagination while exploring these same reptilian manipulatives. He repetitively created and resolved social scenarios using the small toys as actors. Simultaneously, he moved the items into various configurations and groupings. He was later able to describe to me the attributes and reasons he used to sort the objects. If I could just step back and watch, I would see children independently engaging in any number of learning experiences, including mathematical concepts (sorting by attributes, geometric configurations, etc.).

I continued to observe a great deal within the realm of children setting their own difficult challenges, especially when I included our new materials in what I had now dubbed in my mind as "exploratory" small-group rotations. This meant that I chose any combination of the play materials for students to use as they wished (sometimes with, sometimes without my observations and questioning in the background). In addition, the same sets of toys would be available during Self Selection (student choice, self-selected play time) along with the usual Self Selection centers that included blocks, "Home Living," puzzles and games, arts and crafts, and writing. This was an exciting time for me and my students. The classroom was abuzz with children experimenting, collaborating, and negotiating with one another.

As I continued to share my observations with the *Teaching Out Loud* group, group facilitator Katy Crawford-Garrett reminded me that part of our inquiry included documenting and sharing our experiences with our respective communities. I struggled with this in that I was unsure as to how children's play could yield something "presentable" to the community. How could kindergarteners demonstrate learning through play when most of it needed to be observed in the moment and couldn't be staged or produced into something? Katy suggested the use of photographs to allow children to document and reflect on their learning. According to Mincemoyer (2011), "There is a sense of magic a photograph can elicit: Adults have all seen the magic that occurs when a child observes himself in a photograph. It is as if he climbs outside of himself and into the photograph to discover more information" (p. 1). I began photographing the students at play and displaying photographs on the classroom walls. The students were ecstatic with daily requests that I photograph them while playing and creating.

While I didn't experiment with them for long, photographs became a motivational and transformational tool in the case of two students, Tyler and Holly. These two were not typically drawn to one another during play or otherwise. Tyler had experienced challenges in making friends since the beginning of the year. He often struggled to share and take turns and was prone to yelling and aggression when peers responded negatively to him. Tyler was one of four children in his household where his aunt and his older cousin were his primary caregivers. It had taken months for me to establish a foundation of trust and safety with Tyler. He had begun to show some progress with his peer relationships. Despite this, Holly, a quieter child who generally got along with everyone, rarely had the patience for Tyler and often avoided him all together.

One day, Tyler and Holly were both excited to play with our new Zoo-Ominoes (see Figure 4.1). This domino set had become a popular play item due to some unique aspects such as a colorful jungle theme, obstacles, and a mini ball track. As the two children worked on their respective domino projects they chatted excitedly and even gave one another feedback. They demanded that I take photos of their creations. Several times throughout, one of them would accidentally bump the table, knocking down one another's

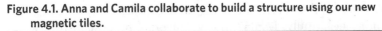

Figure 4.1. Anna and Camila collaborate to build a structure using our new magnetic tiles.

Figure 4.2. Tyler and Holly work side by side using Zoo-Ominoes.

creations. This caused some conflict and disagreement about whose fault it was. At my suggestion, they agreed to move to the floor but, much to my surprise, still wanted to be right next to one another. Byrnes and Wasik (2009) found that children "learned such important skills as the concept of self, patience and turn-taking" (p. 243) when photography was used as a learning tool. Later, I showed Tyler a photo of his time playing next to Holly. He smiled and seemed happy about seeing this moment documented. I hoped that he was beginning to think of himself as a good friend and a real part of our classroom community.

It wasn't as though my classroom was suddenly full of miraculous moments where children were directing their own learning with ease and getting along beautifully. I didn't always integrate purposeful play where I could have, my classroom sometimes felt out of control and chaotic, and children still brought the evidence of trauma to school with them each day. I continued to experiment with my new schedule and priorities. At times, I struggled to embrace unstructured and semi-structured play time. How I thought it looked to outsiders and how it felt was a source of discomfort for me. However, I was making space for my students to find their way, to try, to negotiate, and to be in charge of something. I recognized that my discomfort was liminal and something I could grow from as I learned how to share control. When looking back at our *Teaching Out Loud* meeting transcripts, I recognized that I was rounding a corner. I voiced that "I've just given myself full permission to say, 'this is learning.'"

THE PANDEMIC HALTS THE BEST-LAID PLANS

By the end of February 2020, my inquiry project was beginning to grow legs. In fact, my goal had shifted from introducing more playtime into the day to how best to use photographs to document and share student play projects. I had just begun considering how to collaborate *with* my students to build a photo gallery of play moments and how to best share them with our school community. Then, in the blink of an eye, the COVID-19 pandemic shuttered APS buildings for the remaining months of school as well as the majority of the 2020–2021 school year.

As learning and instruction became virtual, so did the work of *Teaching Out Loud*. In the spring of 2020, we met simply to check in on one another, talk about how our lives had shifted, and share our struggles in adapting to being online teachers. Our meetings were integral in normalizing my own struggles. *Teaching Out Loud* member Kahlil talked about his own son's struggles to engage in online kindergarten, which made me feel seen in my many failed attempts as a teacher trying to make virtual kindergarten interesting.

Our *Teaching Out Loud* work during the 2020–2021 school year continued in much the same way as we navigated the still new world of virtual teaching and learning. However, the months leading up to this new school year had been wrought not only with the continued pandemic, but growing social unrest regarding racism in America. Zacharek (2020) summarized, "in May, the killing of George Floyd at the hands of police in Minneapolis ignited righteous anger not just across the country but around the world. The ruthlessness of that act revived attention to similar outrages earlier in the year, particularly the killings of Breonna Taylor and Ahmaud Arbery. It also reminded us how often, throughout history, Black people had suffered similar injustices, with no recourse, no means of changing the status quo" (para. 9).

These injustices influenced *Teaching Out Loud* conversations as we grappled with how to continue, adjust, or completely change our inquiry projects in response to the impact these events had on the world and our immediate community.

SHIFTING GOALS

In response, our *Teaching Out Loud* work pivoted. We read about antiracist principles, discussed, digested, and eventually, Katy asked us to consider antiracist concepts as we thought about how to move forward with our projects. I felt that preserving play in the kindergarten classroom was a social justice issue. However, I really struggled with how I might link this goal to specifically antiracist principles. Furthermore, how would I promote learning through play in a virtual environment?

Teaching Out Loud continued to be a support for me as I processed these questions throughout the first year of the pandemic and remote teaching. When reading through our meeting transcripts from fall 2020, it seems I grappled with how to adapt my inquiry project while also reflecting on my role as teacher in a virtual world:

> [My revised project idea] is kind of piggybacking off the play [theme] from last year and reframing my role as the teacher, as being the keeper of the knowledge and that, without me, these kids aren't going to learn. And so, I'm hoping to work more on maybe using peer support in creating opportunities to explore, problem-solve, socialize and just kind of like setting the stage for [my project]. It's all about shifting the view of children as "in need," when they arrive. They're not in need of catching up. They're not in need of my help, necessarily. They're not in need of rigor and structure. They're not vessels waiting to be filled.

Was I simply overwhelmed by the prospect of teaching kindergarten with only virtual tools? My words indicated that I was becoming aware of how little control or influence I had over student learning while online. I struggled with how to let go of my expectations and attachments to the traditional school environment while also holding on to hope that these children would be okay without it.

During this same meeting, Katy pressed me, "So how does your project attend to more than just skills-based instruction and how can you address the antiracist principles in the work you're doing? So, a big question, but an important question to be talking about." I didn't have an answer, but Katy's question underlined something I had been hinting at throughout our meetings: I craved permission to deprioritize skills-based instruction in order to offer a virtual kindergarten that provided some relevant morsel to my children and their families given their current circumstances. In getting to know this new group of children, I learned that, due to the pandemic, some parents had lost jobs while others attempted to work from home and also manage their children's remote schooling in the background. Several students connected to class meetings from bustling day cares with limited staff. Grandparents had taken over child care for one of my students, and therefore they took on schooling duties too. A mom brought her two children to her job at a care facility. Her employer allowed her to set up a workspace for them in the staff break room where she would check on them in between work duties. One family was homeless and, understandably, barely able to remain on our school's radar. Device issues and Internet connectivity were a prevalent challenge for nearly every family or day care. As their most convenient yet unqualified source of support, I was suddenly thrust into providing tech support for families.

Many of my students were isolated with adults during this time. Opportunities for peer connection were limited or nonexistent. Furthermore, I had precious few minutes with them during our virtual class meetings before I would lose their attention or connectivity and device issues took over. I continued to find that the virtual stage had major limits when it came to teaching kindergarten academics. I found that students with adult support at home were more likely to log on to class meetings and access academic material via digital assignments. Other students were on their own and did not have an adult who was able to help manage our meeting schedule or assignments. Both scenarios were completely out of my control, and I felt I made little headway when attempting to provide equity in academic exposure. Thoughts about how to spend class time online were prevalent, especially because I generally felt my lessons were a flop.

I spent the remaining months of remote kindergarten experimenting and yielding more of our class meetings to the students. This included having "free time" to talk, show and tell, play games, and sing. Over time, more children participated in these meetings, and there were even some moments that seemed genuinely fun. During one "free time" meeting, only Allie and Taleisha showed up. They spent much of their time together showing their favorite toys; talking to, at, and over another; and eventually "playing" much in the same way that two younger children might engage in parallel play: side-by-side, each engaged in their own tasks, with an occasional, "Look at this" or narrating their play to one another. It didn't look like the play-based learning I had begun to see in the physical classroom, but it was time and space in the day for these kids to access friendship and community.

I provided opportunities for parents and day cares to upload photos of free time and play at home or day care (see Figures 4.3 and 4.4). I put these

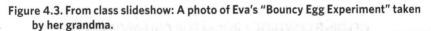

Figure 4.3. From class slideshow: A photo of Eva's "Bouncy Egg Experiment" taken by her grandma.

Figure 4.4. From class slideshow: Peter and his grandma work together to create "snow" in their kitchen.

photos and screenshots taken during our class meetings into a growing slideshow displayed at the beginning of our class meetings throughout the week. This digital "photo wall" allowed the students a glimpse into one another's lives and evidence of themselves and each other engaging during class time. This was my virtual version of using photographs in the learning environment, this time with the aim of reflecting back to the children that they were important members of their virtual community.

YIELDING CONTROL = ROOM FOR COLLABORATION

Collaborating with *Teaching Out Loud* on inquiry-based teaching before and during a pandemic emboldened me to right-size my goals as an educator. Through the ongoing process of questioning, experimenting, discussing, reflecting, and revising, I discovered that one of my biggest challenges in the classroom is to let go and back off in order to better observe, respond, and realize my compassion for my students. Sadly, my early experiences were fraught with educational mandates and punitive reform. This took precious time and energy away from me learning how to appreciate and respond to the humanness of each child I served. I was influenced to fear the implied risk associated with deviating from the rules and my teaching "to-do" list.

In hindsight, I now realize how little control I actually had in the beginning of my teaching career.

The illusion of control was brought into question again as I embarked on an inquiry project that stationed children as powerful in the learning process. Integrating play back into my kindergarten classroom meant taking many deep breaths and growing my patience with myself, my students, and the process I was working to develop. I decided to trust that opportunity and time would yield simultaneous social-emotional and academic growth. That one could not exist without the other. José, Tyler, and several other students were even beginning to demonstrate some of the fruits of my efforts.

Teaching remote kindergarten during a time fraught with incredible fear and unrest (Zacharek, 2020) necessitated that I further embrace flexibility in all realms. It is a lesson I must realize time and again. Many things are out of my control. The best I can do professionally is to hone my skills as an observer and facilitator in search of spontaneous, meaningful, and collaborative learning moments for my students. There are adages about talking less and listening more that pop into my head when I think about these goals. I hope this notion echoes throughout the remainder of my career as I work to focus on the well-being of my students as much as their academic goals.

Looking back at our work together, our own *Teaching Out Loud* group was a model of what meaningful and collaborative learning can look like. As the longest-serving *Teaching Out Loud* members, Katy, Amanda, Damon, and Kahlil, worked to provide goals and structure for our meetings, the content was left to its participants. As we shared our realities as educators and human beings, the often-moving targets of our respective inquiry projects (especially given the circumstances of the pandemic) necessitated flexibility. As I reflect on the deep learning and connections that result from this flexibility, I am reminded that, in all elements of life, the control that I do have is to work to be open, responsive, and flexible.

MOVING FORWARD

Fumbling through creating a virtual kindergarten during a pandemic required that I attempt to partner more than ever with student families. In doing so, I was reminded that each caregiver holds their own preconceptions about the notion of "kindergarten." I got the sense that some families revered kindergarten as a child's entry into serious academic territory. For example, one parent sat next to her child during each class meeting, making sure she was engaged and participating. She often requested more assignments and specific assignments for her child to address the goal of teaching her child to read. Conversations with other families indicated that they were simply grateful for class meetings as a time for their respective child to have social interactions with other kids.

I have always valued parental involvement and communication; however, prior to the pandemic, I had provided few structured opportunities for families to share their thoughts about what kindergarten represents to them. I haven't done enough to engage with and honor the perspective of the family, the parents' preconceived notions based on their own elementary school experiences, or their hopes and dreams for their child. As I reflect on my conversations with families, I wonder how to best open up this type of communication in order to honor parent experiences and expectations. How do I integrate the experiences and ideas of the family into my classroom while also pursuing my goal of "backing off" or balancing academics with child development goals? How do I paint the picture for families that childhood in the public school system is a precarious balance between tending to developmental needs and academic expectations? My goal going forward is to partner with parents while shifting the focus from academic rigor in kindergarten in favor of spotlighting the role of play in healthy child development and learning.

NOTE

1. All student names are pseudonyms.

REFERENCES

Allee-Herndon, K. A., Roberts, S. K., Hu, B., Clark, M. H., & Stewart, M. L. (2021). Let's talk play! Exploring the possible benefits of play-based pedagogy on language and literacy learning in two Title I kindergarten classrooms. *Early Childhood Education Journal*, *50*(1), 119–132.

Byrnes, J., & Wasik, B. A. (2009). Picture this: Using photography as a learning tool in early childhood classrooms. *Childhood Education*, *85*(4), 243–248.

Contreras, R. (2020, January 15). New Mexico child poverty ranking back to 49th in nation, Kids Count report finds. *Las Cruces Sun-News*. https://eu.lcsun -news.com/story/news/local/new-mexico/2020/01/15/new-mexico-kids-child -poverty-ranking-back-49th-kids-count/4481459002/

Felitti, V. J., Anda, R. F., Nordenberg, D., Williamson, D. F., Spitz, A. M., Edwards, V., Koss, M. P., & Marks, J. S. (1998). Relationship of childhood abuse and household dysfunction to many of the leading causes of death in adults. *American Journal of Preventive Medicine*, *14*(4), 245–258.

Gay, G. (2007). The rhetoric and reality of NCLB. *Race Ethnicity and Education*, *10*(3), 279–293.

Gonzalez, J. (2013, November 13). Conquering National Board Certification (and why it's totally worth it). Cult of Pedagogy. https://www.cultofpedagogy.com/nbct/

Griffiths, M. D. (1994). The role of cognitive bias and skill in fruit machine gambling. *British Journal of Psychology, 85*(3), 351–369.

Mickelson, E. L. (2019). The-effects of play-based learning on behavior and academic progress in the kindergarten classroom. [Doctoral thesis, Baker University]. http://www.bakeru.edu/images/pdf/SOE/EdD_Theses/Mickelson _Erica.pdf

Mincemoyer, C. C. (2011). Photographs: Meaningful uses in early education and care. Better Kid Care. http://bkc-od-media.vmhost.psu.edu/documents/TIPS0712.pdf

Özdoğan, E. (2011). Play, mathematic and mathematical play in early childhood education. *Procedia—Social and Behavioral Sciences, 15*(6), 3118–3120.

Repko-Erwin, M. E. (2017, August 23). Was kindergarten left behind?: Examining U.S. kindergarten as the new first grade in the wake of No Child Left. *Global Education Review.* https://ger.mercy.edu/index.php/ger/article/view/324

Smith, O. (2018). The importance of a simple environment. *Montessori Life, 30*(1), 60–60.

Yogman, M., Garner, A., Hutchinson, J., Hirsh-Pasek, K., Golinkoff, R. M., Baum, R., Gambon, T., Lavin, A., Mattson, G., Wissow, L., Hill, D. L., Ameenuddin, N., Chassiakos, Y. L. R., Cross, C., Boyd, R., Mendelson, R., Moreno, M. A., Redesky, J., Swanson, W. S., Hutchinson, J., & Smith, J. (2018). The power of play: A pediatric role in enhancing development in young children. *Pediatrics, 142*(3), 2018–2058.

Zacharek, S. (2020, December 5). 2020 tested us beyond measure. Where do we go from here? *Time.* https://time.com/5917394/2020-in-review/

CHAPTER 5

Creating Conditions for Kindness in a 2nd-Grade Classroom

Kristen Heighberger-Ortiz

My story begins while I was student-teaching in Rio de Janeiro. I had been through all the mandatory education classes, observed teaching strategies in multiple classrooms, tutored in numerous subject areas, and I felt ready. I met my teacher-supervisor, and she gave me all the academic information about the 2nd-graders I would be working with. I knew their reading levels, their strengths and weaknesses in math, and their abilities and interests in science and social studies. I had written detailed lesson plans and walked into the classroom ready to educate. To my surprise, one student, Maria (all names are pseudonyms), had very different plans for the classroom. A few hours into the day, this student began throwing things, tearing up other students' papers, and whispering and yelling uninitiated insults at other students and myself. I was in shock. My carefully developed educational plans were being disrupted by a 7-year-old.

As weeks passed and I talked to the teacher, other teachers, and the principal, no one had an answer for me. I repeatedly heard statements like "She is difficult"; "She has always been like this"; "Her family is kind but not involved"; "She's smart, she'll be fine, don't let her bother you"; "Nothing seems to work with her"; and "She doesn't care about learning."

Eventually, the school counselor suggested that I partner Maria with another student. At first, this did not work, but after several tries and my help in guiding conversations and activities during their interactions, I noticed improvement. It took time, but eventually the two got along and even started to build a friendship. They worked together, and Maria began to see that someone cared about her. She also began taking on a leadership role with the other student, Ashley. I sensed that she felt strong, cared about, and important. An unintended outcome also began to emerge: Ashley was benefiting from the relationship as much as Maria. She was a shy and caring student who was able to show her care and empathy to someone who needed it. Maria was slowly, with help, learning how to accept others and treat others with respect. Ashley was being allowed to exhibit her strengths in a positive, beneficial way. Both students were happy. Both students felt important. Both students felt needed. Both students began to feel more comfortable in the classroom and, in turn, have more success with their academics.

Soon after the two students began to show their success, I had to travel home. I still think about those two students often and wonder what became of their friendship and their academics. Were they able to continue to help each other succeed? Did they ever realize what important part they played in each other's lives? Were they able to continue growing socially and academically? Were they able to pass along what they had done with each other to anyone else?

As my teaching career continued, I saw many students who reminded me of Maria. I taught grades K, 1, 2, and 3 at a variety of different schools. Some schools were large, some were tiny, some were filled with mostly well-off families, some were high-poverty schools. At every school, I repeatedly saw students suffering and, at times, acting out because they wanted someone to care about them or someone to play with them or someone to be with them. Sometimes these needs presented themselves in the form of bullying, sometimes as defiance, sometimes as clinginess, sometimes as being introverted, sometimes as sadness. Young students are in the process of learning how to react to their feelings and emotions. They need guidance, acceptance, and love from adults but also from their peers.

Throughout my years of teaching, I repeated the partner technique that had worked so well with Maria. Sometimes it worked like a charm, and sometimes it was a complete failure. Sometimes the relationships I tried to foster lasted only 10 minutes, and other times long-lasting friendships were formed. Sometimes when asked, the kids were willing, and sometimes I got eye rolls and unpleasant groans. The great thing was that when it worked, positive results in and out of the classroom ensued. The successes were worth the time and effort that needed to be put into the partnerships that began as failures.

When I paired kids up, it was because I saw an emotional, academic, or social need in the classroom. However, one of the most important times for some kids is recess. Kids need the same feeling of acceptance on the playground as well as in the classroom in order to succeed. I tried assigning partners for recess, but most times this resulted in accidental or purposeful separations. This seemed to make problems worse. I could not have the same physical presence on the playground as in the classroom and needed another method to help my students. How could I use the partnership technique at recess to help students learn to be kind and respectful towards others?

TEACHING BEYOND THE TEXTBOOK

At the beginning of the 2019–2020 school year, I found myself, a middle-aged, White woman, teaching in a 2nd-grade English as a second language (ESL) classroom at Nopal Elementary, a Title 1 elementary school with approximately 400 students. My 19 students came from varying backgrounds, including Native American, Hispanic, and White. Several students received special education services ranging in time from 1 hour a day to 5 hours a day. Some students were intermittently homeless, while others were home affluent. Parental involvement also varied greatly with a wide range of support and guidance. Several students were coping with matters not common to "typical" 2nd-graders such as questioning their gender identity or living in foster care. The challenges the students were facing accentuated previously seen social issues, and the need I felt to assist the students in handling these was an ever-present thought in my head. I had always used many different teaching strategies in my classroom but was feeling the need to increase my social emotional knowledge in order to successfully increase and incorporate its benefits in my classroom. I wanted to help my students successfully maneuver their way with their own social emotional matters that were present in their lives.

At the start of the school year, I was given the opportunity to join a group called *Teaching Out Loud*. *Teaching Out Loud* consisted of eight professional and exceptional teachers from around the city who were committed to delving into their practice. I had heard about this group from Amanda, as she was already participating in it. I brought up my concerns with her and asked if she thought the group might be able to help me help my students. She said she wasn't sure, but she did know that the group had helped her professionally and emotionally, and she knew each member would do their best to help me. Once I joined, I was able to see for myself the dedication, commitment, and intelligence of the group members. We met once a month and had assignments and discussions on our own in between our formal meeting times. Each meeting and discussion were enlightening and inspiring. Teachers shared real-life classroom situations with the goal of considering how best to support their students.

The group helped me identify that the problems I was seeing and struggling to solve with my students were rooted in social-emotional learning (SEL) habits. My questions led to meaningful discussions that then led to myself and other members recommending and reading articles and accounts of SEL classrooms. We grew together as we learned together. We explored and learned the importance of SEL in education and human development. We learned how aspects such as applying skills, developing healthy attitudes, managing emotions, achieving goals, establishing relationships, and making responsible decisions are all part of SEL.

According to CASEL (Collaborative for Academic, Social and Emotional Learning), "SEL is the process through which all young people and adults acquire and apply the knowledge, skills, and attitudes to develop healthy identities, manage emotions and achieve personal and collective goals, feel and show empathy for others, establish and maintain supportive relationships, and make responsible and caring decisions" (para. 1).

Throughout the next 2 years, *Teaching Out Loud* helped me dissect what SEL means and work with my students to improve their SEL. My fellow group members reminded me of the benefits of different media such as poetry and art that could be used to work through and engage social-emotional needs.

One particularly helpful discussion revolved around a project Amanda did with her students in which her students created a self-portrait that depicted their personal heritage, feelings, and emotions and wrote a short description about their artwork. I currently had a sibling of one of these students, and the insight about the brother's home life and past experiences gave me insight into my student. I learned of the responsibility that was placed upon my student and his brother. As a result, I was moved and inspired to include more artwork within my teaching. We used watercolors to create self-portraits, designed personalized name plates, crafted jewelry for loved ones, and used clay to mold important objects in our lives. Some of the most inspiring work was done on days when I would put out a variety of art supplies and the students could create anything they chose. My students' artwork gave me insight into my students' lives. Discussions were had and bonds were formed that otherwise may have been overlooked.

Through talking with my *Teaching Out Loud* colleagues, I began to notice that others had recognized the importance of SEL for a while. A middle school teacher in our group shared several emotional stories of students reacting to fictional stories being read in class. The connections made between the books and real-life events were deep and meaningful to the students. According to their 5th-grade teacher, it gave them a reason to talk through personal experiences that in turn helped them process and come to terms with difficult issues such as death and abandonment. Each group discussion made me more and more aware of the need for SEL in all grade levels. As I began my own research process, I realized that some had criticized SEL, calling it a fad and a hoax. I was eager to decide for myself. To begin my learning, I started with the hxstory and background of SEL.

SEL was first conceptualized in the 1960s, when James Comer established the Comer Process. This process focuses on fostering supportive relationships between peers as well as others. This process was piloted in two schools with positive results, including an increase in grades and academic achievement as well as a decrease in behavior issues. This study opened the door for others to see the importance of SEL within schools. More funding became available, and community leaders and foundations began supporting the process and desired outcomes of SEL learning.

SEL has grown, changed, and developed over time. According to the CASEL framework, SEL has five components: self-awareness, self-management, social awareness, relationship skills, and responsible decision-making skills. The fact that community leaders and foundations had an interest in SEL was encouraging to me, but I am not a corporation, foundation, community leader, or school counselor that could begin teaching a formal SEL program. However, the more I learned and the more I taught, my belief in the importance of SEL grew stronger. I felt that being a teacher gave me an inside look at kids and the ability to see them and what they needed. I wanted to use my personal teaching experiences to develop a set of approaches and tools that would help my students and the school community. I took the five key components mentioned earlier, condensed them, tweaked them, and put them into kid language and began. The terms and phrases that I often used with my students were you are a great person and have the ability to help others; not everyone is like you, but everyone has great qualities; everyone needs help sometimes; and simply, be nice!

Building on the principles of SEL and my objective to support students specifically during recess time, I developed a kindness project. The year-long project would culminate with my 2nd-graders constructing a buddy bench for our playground. The benefits of the bench would begin as we began to build it. As a class, we would learn how to paint, hammer, and put together a bench. The end product would be something we could be proud of. Before, during, and after building, I would facilitate discussions about how the bench would give all students someone to play with at recess and how it would avoid the feeling of loneliness that some students experienced during unstructured parts of the school day. We would discuss how everyone felt lonely sometimes and a common way to make someone not lonely was to play with them. I would explain to the students that each recess, two students would be the Buddy Bench leaders. The leaders' job would be to sit on the bench during recess and wait for someone who could not find a friend to play with to come to the bench. One of the leaders would then ask them to play, and together they would find an activity to do. SEL lessons that had revolved around books, activities, and games would be put into practice, with my students helping others feel accepted and cared about. Once we were confident and had practiced different scenarios using the bench, our class would teach 1st-graders, other 2nd-graders, and 3rd-graders how to use it properly. Once everyone understood the bench and how it worked, we would place the bench on the playground and begin putting it to use. This chapter will tell the story of this project and highs and lows that my class encountered along the way.

THE START OF THE SCHOOL YEAR THAT NO ONE EXPECTED: AUGUST 2019–MARCH 2020

I chose to begin my kindness project without telling my students we were doing a project. I did this for several reasons: (1) a year-long project is daunting for 7-year-olds to comprehend; (2) I wanted to get a feel for my students and their social-emotional selves before I jumped into something large; (3) I wanted to teach the components and ideas as a way of life, not as a lesson that can be forgotten or ignored later; and (4) I needed to establish a caring and trustworthy environment before I could ask my students to be caring and trustworthy towards others. To begin creating a caring and trustworthy classroom, we needed to get to know each other. This is a process that begins the first day of school but continues all year. We form bonds by playing games, role playing, working together, and making choices together. The personalities, strengths, weaknesses, needs, and wants are apparent in these activities. I remember watching my students play a game where they tried to find differences and similarities among themselves. They were laughing and having a good time, and as I listened to their conversations I thought about how different and unique each student was. They didn't know it, but as they made these connections, they were reinforcing and enacting living examples of Maya Angelou's sentiment that "in diversity there is beauty and there is strength." I was excited for them to pass this on to others.

As the year continued, I found myself in a classroom of caring, loving, accepting, open-minded students. We had typical difficulties such as bullying and peer pressure, but the students were willing to learn and grow and wanted to make our classroom and school a better place. An example of this revolved around one student in the class who was very open about his past hardships and his temporary placement with a foster family. Twice throughout the year, he excitedly announced that he was going to be adopted. He shared details about his new family to anyone who would listen. Both of these times, the adoptions fell through, and he was extremely upset. Without prompts, many students in our class hugged him and made him cards and notes to cheer him up. They stood behind him during some of what I imagine were the toughest times of his young life. I was sorry the class couldn't join in the Zoom adoption that finally did take place during COVID-19.

USING LITERACY TO FOSTER KINDNESS

As a 2nd-grade teacher, literacy has always been an essential part of my teaching. I love books, and I love seeing students engage with books. I enjoy reading books of all genres and all subjects, but in light of my broader project, I found books related to SEL. Sometimes we would do projects with the books, but most often, I found that after reading an emotional book, the kids just wanted to talk. At the time, *Teaching Out Loud* was reading the book *Puzzling Moments, Teachable Moments: Practicing Teacher Research in Urban Classrooms* by Cynthia Ballenger (2009). During one meeting we discussed a part of the book that focused on the benefits of letting students express their thoughts, ideas, and experiences in their own words and how much they can learn from each other during these discussions. Ballenger states that "children have their own ways to approach new tasks and understanding" (p. 79) and through doing this out loud, they learn from each other. The books we read in my classroom offered an opportunity to apply this strategy. It was easy for the students to relate to the experiences in the books, as they had experienced similar problems. They felt the pain and the joy the characters were feeling. Their student-led discussions taught them that they could relate to each other even when they had previously thought they didn't have anything in common. This was an ongoing process, and each discussion brought up new ideas and connections among the students.

One book that had an exceptionally big impact was *The Recess Queen* by Alexis O'Neill (2002). The book tells the story of Mean Jean, a classic playground bully. One day a new student joins the class, and she doesn't know about Mean Jean. She begins playing when she wants and how she wants. She eventually asks Mean Jean to jump rope with her. Jean is hesitant, but another student encourages her, and she ends up having a great time. From then on, the playground is a much happier, friendlier place. After reading the book, my students had many bully stories to tell. However, after a while, they began to talk more about Mean Jean. They said things like, "It's sad she doesn't have any friends" and "People should be nice to her." We talked a lot about how one invitation to play or one compliment can make someone happy and included, even if they are having a bad day. We also discussed how easy it is to engage in kindness and how everyone is capable of showing kindness to others. The talk was leading perfectly into my plan for the Buddy Bench, but we weren't ready for that yet. I wanted the kids to experience first-hand on a smaller scale how easy it is to make someone feel good. I discovered the book *Kindness Snippet Jar* by Diane Alber (2019). The book has the simple message that being kind can make others feel good. After reading the book and discussing the small things everyone can do to make others happy, we decided to make our own Snippet Jar. This was a place where kids would write compliments to anyone in our class and put them in a jar. We would read them aloud every few days and then hang them up in the hall or in our classroom. This was a huge success! The kids loved writing compliments and beamed with pride both when we read what they had written and when someone wrote them a compliment. One student made a point of asking me who hadn't received a snippet. The next few days she made a point of writing a snippet to the students who hadn't received one. At first, I read the snippets aloud whenever we had time. After a while, I learned that it was great to end the day, especially bad days, with these positive thoughts. After reading the snippets, we put them together to make a collage that hung in our classroom and the students frequently read them during their free time.

Sharing the snippets with the *Teaching Out Loud* group gave me inspiration to continue this project throughout the year. A fellow group member said the snippets were "moving and beautiful." Another stated that it was great to see former difficult students participating in a kindness project. Another complimented the phonics skills that were being put to use.

One other book that I used successfully with my class was a book I have loved since I discovered it many years ago, *A Bad Case of Stripes* by David Shannon (1998). This book demonstrates that not everyone is the same; our unique differences are what make us special, and these unique traits should be celebrated.

There are so many wonderful books that focus on the SEL themes I was promoting and emphasizing. We continued to read and reread these books throughout the year. They sparked numerous discussions and fun projects. A few other books that were successful with this group of students were *Try a Little Kindness* by Henry Cole (2018), *We Don't Eat Our Classmates* by Ryan T. Higgins (2018), and *Each Kindness* by Jacqueline Woodson (2012).

Throughout the year, I talked to teachers and staff at schools around the country about how they use their Buddy Bench. I was given tips and ideas about how to make it a success. I had also consulted with a bully prevention school social worker about needs she had seen fulfilled by Buddy Benches in her district. At the beginning of February, I felt we were ready for the next step, and I introduced the idea of the Buddy Bench to my class. The kids were excited yet seemed a little confused. We continued to talk about the idea, and I showed them pictures of other benches at other schools. We talked about why it would be a good idea to have one at our school. We discussed how it would work and how they would be the leaders that made it work. Together, we decided Buddy Bench leaders would wear a specific t-shirt so students could easily find them. We would wear these as we were leading the others and using the Buddy Bench. The excitement and understanding grew with each discussion. I sent home permission slips so the kids would be able to help sand, paint, and build the bench. All but one

Figure 5.1. Buddy Bench boards ready to be assembled into a bench.

permission slip came back within 2 days. We talked to several influential staff members, and they agreed to help us with the bench construction and, later, with whatever we needed to successfully manage the bench. The idea was spreading, and more people at school were onboard and excited. I had been building up to the actual bench for 6 months, and it was finally time to start building! I showed them the pieces of the bench and explained the steps we would follow to make it. We voted on a paint color and got to work. Most of the kids had never sanded or painted before. They were overjoyed to do this work. They took turns and peacefully shared the supplies and followed directions. Everything was painted and drying over our 2 conference days and spring break (see Figure 5.1). We had scheduled a time with the librarian to help us the Monday after spring break.

Unfortunately, due to COVID-19, our hard work and the beautifully painted boards sat in the classroom for the next 12 months.

SCHOOLS SHUT DOWN AND ONLINE LEARNING BEGINS: MARCH 2020–MAY 2020

Although teaching is never boring, a complete school shutdown and an abrupt shift to virtual learning were not realities I had thought I needed to prepare for. My students had come so far. Their respect towards others, their learning how to help others, and their kindness had grown throughout the year. Their academics had also grown by wanting to read and reread the books we read in class. They pushed themselves to read above their level because they enjoyed the stories. This led to reading more books and requests to check out books from our classroom so they could read them at home. Their writing had evolved from writing small kind snippets (see Figure 5.2) to voluntarily writing letters to me, friends, and family members just to make them feel good. They enjoyed coming to school and had just begun a very exciting hands-on project that they were in charge of. I was worried about my students for many reasons. Life as they knew it had been

Figure 5.2. Part of our snippet collage.

turned upside down. During a conversation with a parent, she mentioned how her daughter was missing school life, her friends, and her work and that she didn't feel connected to her normal life anymore. I had to find a way to make the next 8½ weeks meaningful and to continue the SEL characteristics we had developed and improved upon since August. As we logged on, we continued our academics; we also had SEL check-ins and activities that involved choices such as drawing, writing, and emojis to express feelings. We did things like show and tell, games, and read-aloud of favorite books. The kids were adjusting well (at least as well as everyone else). When I asked about the bench and whether they had any thoughts about it now that it was put on hold, I got a range of answers including, "It was a really pretty blue color"; "I was excited to be one of the people that got to help people when they came to the bench"; and "I'm ready to help everyone be nice!" I involved the 3rd-grade teachers and asked if they would be willing to help promote it and continue to involve my 2nd-graders the following year. All of the teachers enthusiastically said yes! Although I was disappointed that we hadn't been able to see the project to completion, I realized that continuing the project next year was a way to keep this year's students involved, for them to help my next year's students become involved, and for the enthusiastic 3rd-grade teachers to help support the project.

DEVELOPING, STRENGTHENING, AND GROWING WITH ONLINE TEACHING AND LEARNING: THE 2020–2021 SCHOOL YEAR

As schools stayed remote the following fall, "classroom" began to take on a different meaning. Students were doing class in bed; kids weren't showing up for class at all; kids were taking care of siblings while in class; some kids were happy to be home; some kids were disappointed; and often, kids were having to take care of themselves. Each student was in a different place, and seeing their home lives and how remote learning was being handled in each household was eye-opening. I saw some wonderful family situations, and I saw others that made me want to bring my kids together and give them a safe place. Obviously, I couldn't do this physically, so I did what I could to help them learn and understand the basic SEL principles that my previous class had focused on all year. I decided to focus on "you are special" and "be nice." I wanted to create a virtual classroom community and thought these were good starting points. In order to accomplish an understanding and living these two ideas, we played games together, shared our homes, danced together, wrote books together, ate lunch together, and shared talents together. I tried all of these activities in different iterations and let students choose and invent new ones. It seemed as if I was constantly trying something new. Some of the activities had moderate success, but nothing seemed to be forming the bond and connection I was hoping for. Oftentimes, the kids would seem excited about an optional activity but then not show up for it. I asked them about this and about why they didn't seem engaged in our activities, but they were also at a loss. Their answers included, "I forgot"; "I just don't want to"; "I don't know"; and "I'll come next time."

I was lost and frustrated. I felt that kids needed a community more than ever. They needed it to feel good about themselves, and they also needed it to succeed academically and socially. I kept trying. The *Teaching Out Loud* group helped me develop new ideas that they had tried or had heard of others having success with. One of the new activities I implemented was having lunch together throughout the week. I ate lunch online with whomever chose to show up. During this time, students could discuss and/or show off anything appropriate that they chose. This was successful with several students who enjoyed the unstructured interaction with others. We had our own spirit week, which led to students having fun planning their crazy hairstyles together before crazy hair day and making connections when they discovered that they played the same sport on sports day. I also began Friday Free Time. This had been easy in the typical classroom setting but proved much harder online. Together we learned games that worked and didn't work. Friday Free Time often turned into students "being the teacher" and teaching the rest of us new games that they had seen siblings play. I tried many new activities, but I also repeatedly did activities that had been done over and over and based the activities on student votes and requests. If I had made the decision alone, we would not have done so many "show and tells," but the kids requested it, and show and tell days had the largest participation. Show and tell was voluntary but by the end of the year, everyone had participated in some way. By watching and facilitating show and tell day after day, I saw that the kids were growing and learning. They were practicing public speaking, they were getting to show off themselves and what made them special, they were finding similarities among themselves and others, they were learning to be kind to others and to appreciate what made others special. They were accomplishing my goals for them on their own, and I was learning about them and the peer culture they live in.

TRYING TO GET BACK TO "NORMAL"

During the winter months, our school board met and discussed for many hours what should happen next. Eventually, it was decided that families would be given the choice for their students to remain online or return to in-person school for the remainder of the year. Since some of our students would be in person and some would remain virtual, we were planning, anticipating, and figuring out yet another way for learning to happen.

On April 5, 11 of my students returned to the classroom, and it felt like the first day of school. I was shocked when the students were immediately friends and helpful towards each other. They didn't have the normal first day quiet jitters. They already knew each other more than I had anticipated. All the show and tells and the other activities had paid off. They were respectful, helpful, and kind to everyone, including other in-person students and the students who had remained online. Even kids that I had heard had had problems in 1st grade had become friends. This was the best "first day" I had ever had.

The next 7½ weeks brought happiness and a peace of mind that the students had grown in all ways during our virtual classroom. My in-person students requested activities we had done online. The online kids who participated continued to request and come to online lunches and free times. Together and naturally the students developed welcome and goodbye rituals with each other. They were kind, helpful, understanding, and responsible to themselves and to others whether online or in person.

KEY LEARNINGS

The students taught me so much that first day back in person. They taught me to not give up. There were many times during remote learning that I had wanted to quit trying and to just teach the basic required academic skills. I knew this wasn't the right thing to do, and thankfully I had small pushes like an email from a former difficult student apologizing for being mean the year before. She gave me hope to continue, and I hoped I was helping these kids like I had helped her. However, the big realization came on that first day with my wonderful students exhibiting their uniqueness and kindness. I will always remember that during hard times and know that sometimes it takes a while to reap the benefits of hard work.

The students also reminded me to listen to them and not get stuck in an "I need to do this because it's what I planned for today" mindset. My students ended up guiding the optional activities, and it made them better people. I truly believe we did so many show and tells because it is what they needed to continue developing their caring attributes. They may not be able to voice why things are helping them, but with small teacher guidance, they choose what they need to do to learn and develop.

I was happy to learn that SEL techniques can successfully be integrated into many academic lessons. My students made unique connections between SEL concepts and other subject areas. During a science unit, one student compared playing with a lonely person to watering a plant by saying "playing with someone makes them feel good and watering a plant makes the plant feel good." This connection was made on their own and showed me that they were understanding both concepts. Math was enhanced by SEL by writing real-life story problems about SEL situations encountered at school and/or at home. Many times, these showed me what students were willing to share and indicated issues they needed help resolving. Often, we would take these stories and together learn math while talking through specific SEL situations.

NEXT STEPS

Next school year brings hope and excitement for my continuously developing SEL classroom. At the beginning of my Buddy Bench planning, I saw it as a year-long project that would continue on in the school but would not be as developed and taught as it was the first year. I now see the benefits that the pre– and post–Buddy Bench SEL activities brought to my classroom and look forward to participating in them from the first day of school onward. There were times I needed help to make sure all the students were learning the concepts I was teaching. Because of this, I am looking forward to working with the 4th-grade teachers and the original Buddy Bench students. This will have many more benefits also, including enhancing the self-management concept by working in a mentor/mentee relationship with older students. Multiple grades working together will also spread examples of the important SEL principles.

Several staff members had previously agreed to help with the bench. I would like to engage these teachers again. I would also like to involve the school counselor in our lessons and initiation of the Buddy Bench once it is on the playground. She would benefit the project because she is familiar with SEL concepts, knows how to teach them to different grade levels, and is familiar with all the students in the school.

The question of how students' social-emotional states will be at the beginning of the 2022–2023 school year remains unknown. The past 2 years have been trying. The different ways COVID-19 was dealt with in the different homes and communities will have an effect on how the students return to school. This will be positive for some students and negative for others. I will need to adapt my project and classroom to the needs of my students. This brings up many questions such as: How will I use my kindness project to fit these new needs? What new issues will my kindness project bring to light, and how can I incorporate these new ideas into my classroom? How will this change my project? What will I do if my project is not as well received as it was when it began over a year ago?

Whatever next year brings, I will continue to find ways to have a positive classroom and school environment that is centered around the same concepts I focused on previously: you are a great person and have the ability to help others; not everyone is like you, but everyone has great qualities; everyone needs help sometimes; and simply, be nice!

REFERENCES

Alber, D. (2019). *The kindness snippet jar.* Diane Alber Art.
Ballenger, C. (2009). *Puzzling moments, teachable moments: Practicing teacher research in urban classrooms.* Teachers College Press.
Cole, H. (2018). *Try a little kindness.* Scholastic Press.
Higgins, R. (2018). *We don't eat our classmates.* Disney Hyperion.
O'Neill, A. (2002). *The recess queen.* Scholastic Press.
Shannon, D. (1998). *A bad case of stripes.* Scholastic Press.
Woodson, J. (2012). *Each kindness.* Nancy Paulsen Books.

CHAPTER 6

Confronting Race, Identity, and Social-Emotional Learning in a 4th-Grade Classroom

Amanda Y. Short

HOW CAN A WHITE LADY TEACH A CULTURALLY RESPONSIVE CURRICULUM?

In fall 2019, I sat in a district training session for a new elementary language arts curriculum. I had just returned from a Fulbright Fellowship in New Zealand and was refreshed and excited to hear about this curriculum—the Language and Cultural Equity Department in my district had specifically picked it, touting its cultural responsiveness. I had spent my time in New Zealand researching culturally responsive teaching and was thrilled that our district seemed to be on the same page.

As soon as the training started, I knew my excitement had been misdirected. I could tell right away that this curriculum was no different than any other Whitestream Curriculum created by a company on the East or West Coast, interested only in profit, far away from New Mexico's cultures and diversity. Most of the texts had to do with the cultures and climates in Europe or the Coastal United States. In the 4th-grade text, there was a single Native American story, a legend about a trickster (in general this fits many New Mexican cultural stories). I was astounded. We have 19 Pueblos (Native American Sovereign Nations) in New Mexico in addition to the Navajo Nation and Apache Reservations, not to mention the many other Native and Mexican peoples who have lived here for generations. Where were their texts? Where were their stories?

This was the birth of my inquiry question: How could I, a White woman from the Midwest, incorporate local stories, both fiction and nonfiction, into my curriculum in ways that represented the nuance and complexity of New Mexican culture?

STRUGGLING WITH MY PLACE AND RACE
AS I RESEARCHED NEW MEXICO HXSTORY

I am not a native New Mexican—in a state where people have tied their ancestors to this land for centuries, this is an important detail. I came to New Mexico from rural Iowa on a postcollege adventure, hoping to find direction in life. It was within my first month of living here that a New Mexican referred to me as a "White girl." Growing up in a small, Midwestern town, we never talked about race. But this instance made me begin to think about how important it was to know about my own race—as a White woman, I am pained to say, this was a new concept.

Over the past 15 years of teaching in New Mexico, this moment has stuck with me. I consistently wondered how students view themselves and how they view race. America's public elementary and secondary schools are marked by a disproportionate number of White teachers. In the 2015–2016 school year, 80% of teachers were White, while 7% were Black and 9% Hispanic. This is in contrast to the increasingly diverse and multicultural student population—Hispanic, Asian, and children of two or more races increased, while both White and Black populations decreased between 2000 and 2017 (NCES, 2019). I struggle with being one of these statistics and feel a strong need to address the cultural differences between myself and the diverse cultures of my classroom.

My original inquiry project came from the puzzling idea of how a White woman could best help students talk about race and culture within a diverse, multicultural context. My initial solution was twofold—to start thinking about my own racial identity and to start looking at some local hxstorical racism with students. To do this, I centered a literacy unit around the essential question: *How has New Mexico's journey to statehood affected the idea of citizenship for people living in this region?*

Before starting this literacy unit, I began on my own journey of learning more about the hxstory of New Mexico's statehood. The more I learned about the events leading up to statehood, the more I reflected on how the racism and cultural identity of that time period still affect the people of New Mexico.

New Mexico met criteria for statehood in 1850 but didn't become a state until 1912. Congress considered its statehood many times during these years, but each time the bill was rejected for similar reasons: "New Mexico was predominantly Hispano, its adults were largely illiterate, and its language and culture were very different from the 'Americans' who were deciding who would join them as a nation" (Linthicum, 2013).

The area of New Mexico in the late 1800s had diverse populations, specifically over one-third of the population was of Mexican descent. Because of this diversity, the debate about statehood was long delayed. The people in favor of statehood began a long campaign to prove their European worthiness to the U.S. Congress. They loudly proclaimed their Spanish-European heritage, calling themselves *Nativo*, indicating their nativity to the area. Emphasizing their Spanish European descent, they argued many people of the area were no different than their Anglo neighbors to the east (Noel, 2011).

In studying New Mexico's repeated denials of statehood, I wanted to illustrate to students the long-standing racism against the people of this place and connect that to the current debate about citizenship—a very present topic in our border state. Specifically, I was hoping to foster a discussion with students about the hxstorical (and racist) idea that New Mexico had no assets, its people lived in mud houses, spoke Spanish, and were illiterate, preventing it from becoming a valued part of the United States (Linthicum, 2013). I hoped this kind of discussion would connect with students' own experiences of racism and/or heritages and cultures. I hoped this would make discussing current racial tensions easier.

Progressing to statehood was a complex time in New Mexico's hxstory. What I hoped was that with this literacy unit exploring statehood, students would gain an understanding and appreciation for their home and cultures and begin to understand their own positionality. I also wanted to use their learning about local hxstorical racism to structure conversations with students about current racism.

During my time researching this unit, and as I began teaching it, our *Teaching Out Loud* group became my support. While developing this project with the very "touchy" subject of racism, what I needed most was my own emotional support. For example, Damon's activity of *drawing while listening to different types of music* really helped me center myself and relax into proceeding with the project. It is exhausting going forward in a place where others seem to ignore this issue. I know much work has been done on decolonizing education (Abolitionist Teaching Network, 2020), but for a Midwestern, White woman teaching in New Mexico, there is not a lot of site-based support. But through Damon's self-care activities as well as the sharing circles that we did, *Teaching Out Loud* helped me move forward.

SCHOOL POSITIONALITY: USING MY PLACE OF PRIVILEGE TO SHED LIGHT ON THE RACIAL INJUSTICES THAT INFLUENCED MY INQUIRY PROJECT

It is worth noting that my school population represents a good cross-section of the cultures in New Mexico. My students are Pueblo, Dine'é, Mexican, Hispanic, and Anglo. Some have newly immigrated, while others have been here for generations. Some live in hotels, while others live in family-owned homes. They have faced the trauma of racial inequalities, poverty, and food insecurity. Yet they all come excited to explore and build and create. They all come wanting to tell their stories. They all come looking for validation and community connections.

Over my 15 years at Nopal Elementary [pseudonym] I have lived through many changes in our national education system, specifically school choice and the charter school movement, as well as the school grading system. This sociopolitical backdrop shaped the content of my inquiry project and continues to influence my approach to teaching.

As school grading and high-stakes accountability trickled down to my school of about 400 students, I have seen our population shift as affluent families fled the school. When the school grading system came to New Mexico, our school was given an "F" letter grade because of our low standardized test scores. Interestingly, low school letter grades across the city correlated with high populations of students who received free/reduced-price lunch. A fellow teacher and activist, Francesca Blueher, created the graphic in Figure 6.1 to illustrate this.

A few notes about this graphic:

- This data is from the school year 2013–2014.
- No district elementary school received an "A."

Figure 6.1. Percent of families receiving free/reduced-price lunch by school grade.

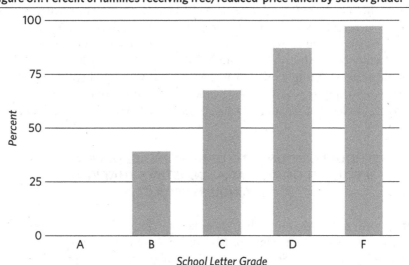

- There were NO *high-poverty* schools (a term that Francesca defines as underserved and underfunded by the federal, state, and local governments) in the category of "B" schools.
- Ten out of the 13 "F" elementary schools have 100% of their families receiving free and reduced-price lunch.

This graphic is not to say that "poor people can't take tests" or that "poor people are lazy," but rather it is an attempt to make the invisible (racism) visible on a local level. Tests have long been used as a racist tool to categorize students and people (Rosales & Walker, 2021). Because school letter grades are directly tied to high-stakes tests, this was no exception. What happened at my school is summed up by Ibram X. Kendi (2021): "Standardized tests have become the most effective racist weapon ever devised to objectively degrade Black and Brown minds and legally exclude their bodies from prestigious schools. . . . The tests have failed time and again to achieve their intended purposes: measuring intelligence and predicting future academic and professional success. The tests, not the black test-takers, have been underachieving" (as cited in Rosales & Walker, 2021, para 5).

Affluent parents saw the "F" designation our school received and fled, missing out on the rich cultures and talents at our school. For example, they didn't see students baking bread in a Horno oven or participating in the Math Olympiad. They didn't witness dynamic class discussions in which students argued from many points of view and in different languages. They didn't see our dance classes and our world exhibition on social studies day. They missed out on a character parade and poetry slam, and they missed out on throwing pies at the principal for Pi day.

When school grades linked to test scores are how we measure a "good school," we forget to reflect on what is truly meant by a good education. As Diane Ravitch (2010) notes in her book, *The Death and Life of the Great American School System*, "The trouble with test-based accountability is that it imposed serious consequences on children, educators, and schools on the basis of scores that may reflect measurement error, statistical error, random variation, or a host of environmental factors or student attributes" (p. 166). I might add that it also detracts from the real problem—the problems that we are unwilling to fix in these underserved "F communities." We do not pour time or money into providing health care, mental health services, quality food, adequate housing, or access to living-wage jobs; instead, we label the school with an "F" and blame the teachers.

At Nopal Elementary, with these changes in population came changes in state and federal curriculum requirements. Low-scoring schools must use specific curricula to "get students caught up," and they must give more standardized tests. With these requirements, teachers are no longer "allowed" (or given time) to create curriculum that fits the population they serve (Moon, et al., 2007); we risk bad evaluations, harsh judgments, and write-ups if we do so. It can be exhausting trying to both fulfill the requirements and create a curriculum that fits students' needs and interests.

I personally faced retribution when advocating for my students by wanting to teach rich, culturally relevant content instead of district curriculum. As a result, I received the following comments on my evaluation:

> The teacher meets the requirements of her teaching position but has had difficulty with being respectful of policies and procedures. I feel that she has had a negative impact on the culture of Nopal [pseudonym] this year. . . . *It has been difficult this year for Amanda . . . because of changes in the district requiring immediate implementation, support, and communication. She has made the conscientious decision to take a stand against new requirements which she cannot support, and this has required the IC (Instructional Council) and I to spend a huge amount of time holding her accountable for the things in which we are also being held accountable for. . . .* (Crawford-Garrett et al., 2016, p. 8)

I want to acknowledge that I come from a place of privilege—I am a White, veteran teacher with little fear of losing my job because of this advantage. I was angered and scared because of this evaluation, but I wasn't alone in my actions and knew that I could stand with others in this fight for a better curriculum and in advocating for my students.

All these situations and events have greatly influenced my teaching and specifically my inquiry project. Because of current events and the current education system, and because of my own experiences with this system, I continue to want to create a curriculum relevant to local issues, cultures, and hxstories. Now, more than ever, we need critically minded students who have developed a healthy sense of self and can advocate for equality.

TALKING WITH STUDENTS ABOUT HXSTORICAL RACISM

To give an idea of the diversity in my classroom, in fall 2019, 32% of my students were Hispanic, 24% White, 12% Pueblo (Acoma, Jemez, and Santo Domingo), 8% Dine'é, 8% Mexican, one student was African American, one from Hong Kong, and one was from the Congo.

I began the year with my New Mexico Statehood and Race inquiry project. Students spent a few months researching events that led up to statehood. They researched the Mexican–American War, industries that became important in the area during that time (mining, cattle ranching), the U.S. Civil War, and events around Native resistance to the European invasion. For my final assessment, I assigned groups of students hxstorical figures to play for a debate in which they argued about wanting to join the United States as a state or not. Students played the parts of Geronimo and the Apache tribe, New Mexico ranchers represented by Billy the Kid, Taos Pueblo leaders, the territorial government officials, New Mexico's delegates to Congress, and New Mexico Governor Marsh Giddings. For the debate I had one student do an outstanding job of portraying Billy the Kid's dislike for law and order from the U.S. government, a reason to not become a state.

As part of their debate prep, I had students watch a short video about Puerto Rico in an attempt to conceptualize the idea of territory. Students knew about Puerto Rico from Hurricane Maria of 2017, and we discussed how devastating this had been. I wondered aloud about why the relief to Puerto Rico had taken so long and was so minimal in general. And then a student brought up the then President Trump's paper towel–throwing incident, and the classroom erupted in chatter.

Next, students explored why people in the U.S. Congress of 1900 (give or take) might call New Mexicans dirty, ignorant people (Linthicum, 2013). I had the students read an article from the local newspaper describing these biases of the time and put it to the students—*why do you think those things were said about our region?* Students thought maybe it had to do with a misunderstanding. I agreed, citing the idea that living in "dirt" houses (adobe) was a great way to survive in the desert.

Following both of these discussions, I attempted to connect the events to racism. We discussed what racism looks like today. I asked students what they thought. Many students gave the typical answer that Martin Luther King, Jr. and Rosa Parks had "gotten rid" of racism. I asked questions about situations that were unfair—like, what do you notice that isn't fair about our school or our city? This was a difficult discussion because most students didn't seem engaged or interested. I would have to revisit this and consider how to better support students to connect the dots and to name the invisible racism endemic to their lives. This emerged as a moment of dissonance for me, one that I would need to revisit in the future. How could I make this discussion more relevant to them? How could I change things to make this a more robust discussion? Would writing about the topic be a better approach? How could I facilitate building knowledge around this complex topic?

CONNECTING STATEHOOD TO SELF

As a way to try to make the statehood project more personal, I decided to add a self-reflection piece. I wanted to create a way for students to reflect on what they had learned about New Mexico hxstory to themselves. I decided to have them brainstorm ways to describe themselves: who they are; their interests; where they come from; and their families, traditions, and cultures. Then I asked students to create a Surrealist self-portrait to reflect these things about themselves (see Figure 6.2). I was hoping that this could tie to race and cultural identity and provide a link to the New Mexico statehood project.

Students took this idea in many different directions—some drew their favorite activities (there were a lot of Naruto references); some drew flags to show their heritage (for example, one student drew both U.S. and Mexican flags); one student drew herself divided, on one side she was speaking English and on the other, Dine'é. Many students saw this idea of a divided self and went with it. Then one student drew about her emotional self, and the class began to collectively build on that idea. As an example of the emotional theme that seemed to be emerging, one student wrote the following about her portrait: "My portrait's meaning is that outside feelings do not show inside feelings. I drew it that way so people struggling would know they are not the only one struggling. I like the drawing because it describes my life. The portrait shows that life can be hard but it's okay because they're not the only one struggling."

I was surprised at the openness and willingness to share about difficult feelings and about emotional needs and struggles. What I hoped would be about racial identity or cultural identity was more about social-emotional identity. This was a turn I had not anticipated. I began to think about how much students are already fluent in social-emotional learning (SEL). SEL is

Figure 6.2. Here are the final Surrealist-style self-portraits from February 2020.

the "new buzz" in education—a good thing to focus on, but like many things in education, the idea becomes mutilated and deformed when coming from the district. SEL refers to the life skills that support people in experiencing, managing, and expressing emotions; making sound decisions; and fostering interpersonal relationships (Simmons, 2019). How could I build on this? Students need a safe venue to discuss and share, not a teacher who tells them what to say or how to say it. I needed to change how I was listening to them. New questions arose: How do students currently talk about their feelings? What stories do they have to tell about experiences with trauma? How can I use the larger sociopolitical context to teach SEL strategies? I am inspired to push myself to change as I think about Dena Simmons's (2019) words, "What's the point of teaching children about conflict resolution skills, if we're not talking about the conflicts that exist because of racism or white supremacy?" Without that nuance, she says, SEL risks turning into "white supremacy with a hug" (as cited in Madda, 2019, para. 10).

I wanted to create a larger venue for students to share their work, so we had an art opening at a public library close to the school. As I prepared for the art opening, I was unsure how to proceed with the display—should I put up the students' artist statements as they were, or should I spend more time correcting the grammar and spelling? On one hand we were representing our school, and I knew people would judge misspellings and punctuation errors. But on the other hand, I wanted students to be able to express their thoughts without the barrier of "being correct." (Side note: In my experience, an emphasis on error-free writing can cause major writers' block and/or a hatred of writing with kids.) I brought this struggle to the *Teaching Out Loud* group, and as I did, I realized how much anxiety I held around this issue. The group encouraged me to let the students' voices be heard without major corrections, just making a note in the display sign that these were more of a free-write. As we discussed my project more, Katy suggested that I also add a way for visitors to reflect on their experiences with the portraits and artist statements and be able to document their feelings about the space. I agreed that this would make the project even more powerful for both the students and the visitors and created a way for visitors to do so.

I invited families, community members, and our school board representative to the art opening (see Figure 6.3). It was well attended. The school board representative was thrilled. She was especially struck by the drawing of the student who showed the languages she spoke—English and Dine'é. She asked me, "Have you talked to the language and cultural equity department about a Navajo language teacher coming to your school?" I had, in fact, already done this. I was told by the district that there weren't enough Diné language teachers to go around, and I should ask a parent to help out.

Figure 6.3. Student self-portraits on display at the public library.

Again, there was a disconnect between those in charge and the actual school, a dismissal of what communities were asking for, and a lack of understanding about the community they serve—an issue that became even more evident with the pandemic.

INQUIRY APPROACHES: TEACHING DURING THE PANDEMIC, STRUGGLE WITH SELF AND MENTAL HEALTH

And then COVID-19 hit, and school life turned upside down. As the months of online school stretched on and the fall of 2020 began with no promise of in-person learning, preexisting social issues were increasingly blamed on schools and teachers—we were to blame for an increase in kid/teen suicide rates, for depression and the mental health needs of students, for the "learning gap" that was developing—the list became endless. Instead of looking at the lack of social programs and health care services, many people simply blamed schools. As an educator, this load became a heavy burden to bear.

I began the 2020–2021 school year by watching an online panel discussion, "Raising Co-conspirators: Talking about Racism with White Kids" hosted by the Abolitionist Teaching Network (2020). The discussion was led by Dr. Bettina Love and included Ronda Taylor Bullock, Torri A. Tosolt, and Cherish Williams. Mentioned in this talk was the idea that just as we teach elementary students about physical health, we should also teach them to have a healthy love of self (not better or worse than others) and a healthy racial identity. I was inspired. I hoped to make this the framework for my school year. I wanted to continue my inquiry project centered around the question: *How has New Mexico's journey to statehood affected the idea of citizenship for people living in this region?* But this time I wanted to be more intentional about developing a healthy racial identity as part of the project.

I was not prepared for the stress of online school. It became almost unbearable. I physically had to drag myself to the office chair where I set up my computer station. Not only was the teaching and learning portion excruciating (take a job that is based on human interaction and remove the human interaction), but suddenly I was intimately a part of every student's home. It is a strange situation to be a part of your students' families and homes. This worked both ways—teachers witnessed more than before and the families witnessed more than before. This added a whole new layer of stress.

I remember an especially difficult moment that came up with a student. I had given students a math puzzle, wanting them to use as many different mental strategies as possible. As we were discussing these strategies, one student said the incorrect answer. And then I heard from the background of his home a person yelling, "Why the fuck would you think that's the answer?!!! Fucking pay attention!"

This was so difficult for me to hear—learning doesn't happen when you are berated for an incorrect answer. I felt so sad for this student, and I needed my own emotional support. Thus, I was happy to have our *Teaching Out Loud* group for this very purpose. When I shared this especially difficult situation, Katy responded with, "It must be so brutal to hear that over Zoom. I can't imagine." I got the emotional support I needed from our group of professionals. Listening to their stories, for example, when Linnea shared about calling Children, Youth, and Families Department (CYFD) not because there was neglect or abuse but because there were no resources for a family in need, I no longer felt as alone. The pandemic made teaching an incredibly lonely job, especially when experiencing traumatic student situations, and I was thankful for the support I found through *Teaching Out Loud.*

As the pandemic progressed, I was at an early morning meeting with the leadership team of my school. I sat bleary-eyed clutching my coffee, staring at my screen. The principal was proposing a new SEL curriculum for us to adopt. He was echoing the growing concern for students' mental health needs to be addressed within the school system. The principal wanted our school to adopt the Accept, Identify, Move (AIM) curriculum—"a behavior analytical curriculum for social emotional development in children" (Paliliunas & Dixon, 2018)—the latest "quick fix" the district was trying out to appease the community's call for more social-emotional supports in schools.

Even in my early morning fog, I began to grow angry. How was this going to solve the situation of my student getting yelled at for coming up with an incorrect answer? How was this curriculum culturally relevant? Where was the racism training that needed to accompany a curriculum like this? With our culturally rich school population, why would we waste time trying to teach Brown and Black students how to talk about their feelings using Whitestream language? It is infuriating sitting through leadership meetings, trying to communicate how much our students need and how much they are missing the mark with these "quick fixes."

As my students demonstrated in their self-portraits, they know how to talk about their emotions; they know how to share and support each other; they know how to advocate. This helped me understand that discussing racism with students looks like discussing their emotions, their stories, validating their way of communicating, and acknowledging that they are hungry to share their struggles in their own way. Although lingering questions for myself as a professional include: How do I help them name racism? How do I build on what they're already able to do? How do I help students translate race from an individual experience to a systemic one? How do I connect their feelings to the underserved (by society) situations they find themselves in? As Dena Simmons (2019) states, "Students need the skills to navigate unjust realities" (para. 1).

During the school year of online learning, I began my inquiry project with every intention of focusing on some of the local hxstorical context of racism. But instead, I focused on ways for students to express their emotional needs. In the times of unprecedented everything, I felt students needing a space to express their feelings. I introduced journal writing. I had students keep a journal about living through COVID-19. As a way of showcasing these journals and motivating the writing of their stories, the entries were submitted to the New Mexico State Archives. I invited a librarian from the New Mexico State Archives to come and discuss the use and importance of archives with our class. The students were excited to have their work in the same place as letters from Billy the Kid.

Most students took to this project with enthusiasm. Throughout the project, I would ask for volunteers to share some of their writing, and often students would read about how scared or sad or lonely they were. A few things that were shared:

"I'm worried about getting sick."

"Dear Diary, 2020 is the worst year ever. I miss my friends. I've lost TWO animals and it's . . . just hard. My dad said, 'point out the good things in life' . . . but the thing is there are almost no good things!"

"I can't believe I'm saying this, but I miss school."

"Today is Halloween! It wasn't as fun as the rest of Halloweens because we couldn't go trick-or-treating, and I couldn't show everyone my costume."

"COVID-19 is the worst! I was going to have a big sleepover for my birthday but that did not happen. Mr. Corona over there has ruined my life for the past several months."

"My dad's work has been considered essential and has been having to work this whole time. I worry for my dad having to work so much but he is my hero! My mom's work has been closed since March and still isn't able to open. . . ."

Through this sharing, students would support each other, echoing and acknowledging these struggles—much like the *Teaching Out Loud* group was for me.

Student sharing of their journal entries and their writing inspired me to again do the Surrealist-style self-portrait project. I thought this could be a great way to finish the COVID-19 journaling project and give students another medium to share their feelings. Like last year's students, they took this in different ways, but many of them used it to communicate their emotional needs. One student explained the project by saying, "We had to draw ourselves on the inside and the outside."

Figure 6.4 is an example of one student's work from this project.

Figure 6.4. Student work.

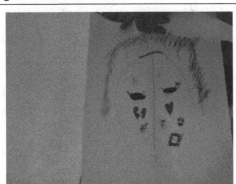

The trees represent how I have been lonely during covid-19.
The board game is because I love playing board games with my family.
The book is because I love reading books.
The dog on the right side explains how I love my family very much as well as the heart.
The dog on the left side explains how I am sad and miss the rest of my family.

Again, the students surprised me at their openness and their ability to express their fears, sadness, joys, and passions. I come back to wondering how can I build on this openness in order to discuss racial inequalities and cultivate positive racial identities?

CALLING FOR CHANGEMAKERS

As I reflect on this year of teaching through a pandemic, I hope we can all agree that social-emotional supports are essential. Students are hurting, they are worried and lonely, they yearn to feel safe and supported and healthy. Many children already use their own language to express these needs. What are we doing to make it an open, safe place for students? The problem comes when teachers are asked to provide remedial classes or curriculum for students who are "behind" because of a pandemic or when teachers are asked to heal trauma without the help of professionals or when teachers are asked to feed and clothe students. If our nation truly wants to solve this problem, then we need to prioritize legislation that funds more school social workers and counselors, housing and food for families, health care, and mental health care. The school cannot provide all of these things without funding. When we spend all our time blaming the school and the teachers, we are blinded and don't see the real issues or real solutions.

As I pursue my own journey in this position of a White teacher in a diverse classroom, working in a dysfunctional system, I want to work toward a culturally responsive SEL curriculum for my students. Dena Simmons (2019) states: "SEL has tremendous potential to create the conditions for youth agency and civic engagement and, ultimately, social change. We owe our students an education that centers on their lives and explicitly addresses the sociopolitical context. This will not only prepare our students to engage civically and peacefully across difference, but also to become the changemakers and leaders we need" (para. 8).

Through the pandemic, my original inquiry question morphed and changed when students focused on social-emotional well-being. The lingering question for me is: How can I better create a culturally relevant social-emotional learning curriculum using local hxstory as a framework?

KEY TAKEAWAYS

As I reflect on my time in the *Teaching Out Loud* group and my inquiry project, a few takeaways come to mind. First, teaching is a challenging profession because we exist in a dysfunctional system—remember, you are not alone. Like our *Teaching Out Loud* group and like my students, create a support group. Work together to preserve your own mental health as you advocate for what's best for students. Find people to share your stories with; laugh and cry together; eat chocolate; encourage each other; and if you partake in alcohol, have a good bottle of wine on hand.

Second, take time to get to know your students. While this seems obvious, what I mean is let them guide you—step off the stage and listen to what they are chattering about. Prioritize what matters to them. For example, my students needed to prioritize sharing about their emotional struggles and their mental health. When you let them guide, they will learn and grow with you. Allow yourself to change as much as your students do over the academic year as you get to know each other.

Next, remember teaching is not about "getting through" the curriculum. Use your place of privilege to advocate for a culturally relevant curriculum. Allow students to cocreate the knowledge of your classroom. If they need to talk about how they are hiding their sadness and loneliness from the world, let them. Put the textbooks away and let them build ideas together. Do what is best for the students, not what is best for the company selling the curriculum. Academic skills will come through this process.

Lastly, support students in developing self-advocacy skills and becoming changemakers. Allow them to have a venue for their voices and then build on that. Let students explain things their way and then push them to expand into self-advocacy and make change. Give students opportunities to become the change. For example, when I had the art opening at the local library, our school board member was confronted with the fact that our district isn't providing the language education she thought.

I will end by asking you as an educator to examine your own positionality: How does your place in the world influence your teaching? How can you make change within our dysfunctional system? How will you guide students to become the voices of change in our country?

REFERENCES

Abolitionist Teaching Network. (2020, August 22). Raising coconspirators: talking about racism with white kids" hosted by the Abolitionist Teaching Network [webinar]. Eventbrite. https://www.eventbrite.com/e/raising-coconspirators-talking-about-racism-with-white-kids-tickets-116271042819

Crawford-Garrett, K., Perez, M., & Short, A. (2016). Leveraging critical literacies for social change: Questioning the culture of compliance at an 'F' school. *Teaching Education 28*(3), 1–17.

Kendi, I. X. (2019). *How to be an antiracist*. Random House.

Linthicum, L. (2013, October 23). New Mexico's path to statehood often faltered. *The Albuquerque Journal*. https://www.abqjournal.com/286241/new-mexicos-path-to-statehood-often-faltered.html

Madda, M. (2019, May 15). Dena Simmons: Without context, social-emotional learning can backfire. EdSurge. https://www.edsurge.com/news/2019-05-15-dena-simmons-without-context-social-emotional-learning-can-backfire

Moon, T., Brighton, C., Jarvis, J., & Hall, C. (2007). *State standardized testing programs: their effects on teachers and students.* The National Research Center on the Gifted and Talented.

Noel, L. (2011). "I am an American": Anglos, Mexicans, Nativos, and the national debate over Arizona and New Mexico Statehood. *Pacific Historical Review, 80*(3), 430–467.

NCES. (2019, February). Status and trends in the education of racial and ethnic groups. https://nces.ed.gov/programs/raceindicators/indicator_RAA.asp

Paliliunas, D., & Dixon, M. R. (2018). *AIM: Accept, identify, move.* Shawnee Scientific Press.

Ravitch, D. (2010). *The death and life of the great American school system.* Basic Books.

Rosales, J., & Walker, T. (2021, March 20). The racist beginnings of standardized tests. National Education Association. https://www.nea.org/advocating-for-change/new-from-nea/racist-beginnings-standardized-testing

Simmons, D. (2019). Why we can't afford whitewashed social-emotional learning. *ASCD Education Update, 61*(4). http://www.ascd.org/publications/newsletters/education_update/apr19/vol61/num04/Why_We_Can%27t_Afford_Whitewashed_Social-Emotional_Learning.aspx

CHAPTER 7

Imagining Joy
Toward Abolition in the Middle School Classroom

Kahlil Simpson

THE INITIAL QUESTION

This is not the story I wanted to tell. When I conceptualized this work, when I planned and, eventually, replanned my school year, I had a different narrative in mind. I thought that my classroom could be a space of respite. Like many teachers, I considered the interior lives of students. The intense isolation they must be facing, possible familial loss, the violence and White supremacy seemingly ever-present in our communities, and I created with this in mind. I put in that familiar work of building a classroom and curriculum that can hold space for and persist in spite of these realities. I considered the triumph of such a space: the powerful story it would tell. I considered the triumph but was met with reality. The reality of the martyrdom within my own practice—that I, too, hurt. The reality that schools do not and cannot love us back. The reality that, in order to seek joy, some things must break.

At the onset of the pandemic, my school was one that did not shut down. As a small charter school, we had enough access (and a small and privileged enough population) to immediately turn to a virtual format. Thus, our school year was encouraged to continue in much the same manner it had done in person: with pushes of "holding students accountable," "rigor," and diagnosing and fixing students by focusing on "lacking skills." At the same time, I watched my friends and partner, like many others, lose their jobs (Richter, 2021), hold, and in some cases skip funerals of loved ones who had passed during the pandemic, and I continued to see people like Breonna Taylor (Elahi, 2020), and George Floyd (Williams, 2020) and so many others, people who look very much like myself or members of my family, murdered. As a result, I felt friction between what I was being told to do and the reality I was living. A friction I can now name as erasure, a normative practice in an educational system that frequently asks both students and teachers to dismiss lived experience from the classroom (hooks, 1994). And in these moments, there is always a point, where we, as teachers, can decide to go along or go in another direction. And at that moment I, and many other teachers in my school, chose the latter. As a result, the 2019–2020 school year finished in a sprinted marathon, creating curriculum from scratch, advocating for humanizing grading practices, learning new systems and ways of doing, calling families and students on personal numbers and at all hours of the day, working all night to ensure that no one student was failed in a pandemic. Teachers do this kind of work. The invisible, the unpaid, and uncredited. And to my surprise we were lauded for it (Ortiz, 2020; Robbins, 2020). However, as the pandemic stretched through the summer of 2020, reality set in that we would be in a similar place in the fall.

At the onset of the 2020–2021 school year, I found myself on a similar ledge. I remember speaking with Amanda, my *Teaching Out Loud* colleague, about this exact dilemma. We discussed what things might need to change in a virtual environment. We wondered what kind of teaching was possible. I specifically recall her asking if this is the year that she "gives in" and teaches out of the textbook. I remember leaving with the same thoughts buzzing in my head. "Is this the year I go along?" The question was there for all educators, and for me it lingered all summer. The real tension was not which decision was the right one, but what was even possible? Could I make it possible? With the road already hard, would it be wise to add new obstacles?

If I am being honest, this—the choice to go against the grain—was the choice I always knew I would make. As a Black biracial educator, I am frequently reminded of my own educational hxstory, and from that I know that I will not perpetuate the same (Simmons, 2021). Thus, I find myself frequently taking that other option: creating new curriculum, new resources, challenging top-down ideas of best practice, centering identity and inquiry in the classroom, and most times going it alone. But as summer quickly became fall, I became aware that I no longer wanted to work alone.

What I found was a need for collectivism. As teachers, the initial shutdown showed us the ways in which we *did* and the ways in which we were *going to* need each other. And in this new push we can also recognize that the ways in which school, as it is presently situated, stands in opposition to this. School promotes a largely individualistic model: teachers are evaluated in isolation of the larger school context, are rarely praised openly—when we are, it is primarily for incredible acts of exceptionalism (e.g., working extra hours, creating new initiatives, generally performing miracles)—and at the same time are frequently reminded that our individuality is a threat to our job security (as exemplified by efforts at standardization and a district-controlled curriculum with failing teachers and schools).

By summer's end, I had gathered a group of teachers and, not quite support, but permission from administration to carry out (virtual) home visits with all incoming 6th-grade students and their families. These visits were in direct response to this push for collectivism. In light of the pandemic, we (two other 6th-grade teachers and myself) realized that this might be the only time we can meet students without the complications that grades and classroom expectations bring. Further, we knew of our own school's insistence on teaching "for real" and the frequent championing of "rigor" and "college prep." We recognized the ways in which these narratives, just as those surrounding our own teaching, seek to divide students. Additionally, we recognized how many students this system of thinking fails. So, my peers and I created a list of questions and topics that we hoped would combat this. The questions themselves were inspired by the work of Luis Moll (Gonzalez et al., 2005), hoping to expand the notions of what information is necessary to know about our students and to shift thinking about students as a whole. In interviewing my co-conspirators, they had a similar realization that we had an opportunity to reframe expectations of school not just in a pandemic but for all time.

With feedback from the school social worker and members of my *Teaching Out Loud* group, we decided to conduct the visits as a group. The three of us gave our students asynchronous work and conducted a visit every 12–15 minutes for 6 hours on Fridays for 3 weeks. The work was exhausting, but in it we got to discuss student interests outside of school, family values, and makeup, and most importantly, we got to frame parents as experts of their child and the education of their children as a partnership. For the first time it felt like I had some agency in the school. In interviewing the others in the group, we all felt a need to do things differently by leveraging our students and families as stakeholders and partners, working in partnership with them instead of diagnosing them and prescribing fixes. We felt a need to carry this momentum forward. So, we did. And as we did, I found my own question: What might this work lead to? In essence, I considered what impact centering students and their families would have on the school, the community, and my teaching.

THE BREAK: CONFRONTING BARRIERS TOWARD CHANGE

For a time, the impact was apparent. We had firsthand information on students and feedback about what parenting and schooling in a pandemic were actually like. We formed a 6th-grade department, when there was never a formalized one before. We created a staff directory for parents to know who and why to contact different staff of the school. We sent home a schedule of asynchronous and synchronous meeting times for all classes and grades in middle school. We advocated for weekly collaboration; student support on Fridays; pushed for discussion about student workload; and developed and collected numerous data collection tools for parents, students, and their remote learning experiences. I found myself in all these conversations I previously was not privy to. For example, I was invited to the table effecting policy and change in the school. But as the year went on, students continued to fail (Land, 2020; Thompson, 2020). Eventually, home visits became not only something 6th-grade teachers did, but something the school did. The erasure of our authorship allowed the school to highlight the ways in which we, a school of choice, was doing it "better" than others. Further, it allowed the school to present this "we care about students" and "we are doing the work in our communities" message the school vision rests upon without being responsible for making tangible changes. Our work became a check box. It was presented as a solved problem so we could go back to the "real" work of grading and accountability.

By the end of the fall semester, I was exhausted. However, my participation in *Teaching Out Loud* and my attendance at National Council of Teachers of English (NCTE) that year, that communion with other teachers, left me rejuvenated and determined. Often it was not until dialoguing with my *Teaching Out Loud* peers that I was able to feel justified in my teaching. Thus, with the first day of winter break, I outlined the rest of the year. I filled chart papers with the changes necessary for the way forward and taped them to my wall. These posters were filled with things like new systems for student interaction, more small-group attention, a more forgiving grading system, with underlines and stars next to words like "visibility," "power," and "access." But when it came time to move towards action, I was stuck. The mood had changed. I couldn't create in the same way. I couldn't suddenly materialize the ability to hold all the parts of a broken system in my hands. The plans stayed plans. They stayed, and remain, taped to the wall in my dining room.

In her profound text, "We Want to Do More than Survive" (2019), Bettina Love discusses Patricia Williams's (1987) concept of "spirit-murder." The term, as Love defines it, is not just the maiming of the physical body by racism but the slow death (read murder) of spirit and humanity caused by White supremacy. Love argues that since racism is a systemic and institutionalized force present in all levels of our society, school, too, is a space impacted by and perpetuating the spirit-murdering of the students they house. The evidence of this assault during the pandemic was apparent. Despite leaving our physical spaces behind, schools continued to disproportionately monitor, suspend (Elfrink, 2020; Grzeszczak, 2020), and even incarcerate Black and Brown students (Cohen, 2020).

This same spirit-murder applies to teachers as well. We were tasked with creating new ways of operating, but at the end of the day were solely responsible for its success or failure. As a teacher, within this same system— one in which I also came up in—I found myself in a similar position. Home visits were a failure. We uncovered a new way to interact and work with students and parents, but our community was essentially left unchanged. As a result, I was exhausted, but more concerning was that my soul was wounded, and I felt unable to dream.

RECONCILIATION BY WAY OF REFLECTION: A RATIONALE FOR MOVING AND IMAGINING FORWARD

The work of Bettina Hsieh (2016) reminds us that educators cannot run from their identities in their role as teachers. We teach who we are. The trauma of working in a crumbling system, the spirit-murder I endured and continue to endure ran me into a wall. But it was through this sudden halt that I began to see myself through new lenses. Trauma can be humanizing (Dutro, 2019), even for oneself; for me, being beset with my own allowed me to see the ways in which I was running from my own hxstory.

As a student I had a tumultuous experience within and eventually out-side of schools. Due to illness, which I now recognize as depression and anxiety, I spent much of my high school career at home. As a young Black man in predominantly White schools, I felt highly visible. My own struggles with finding acceptance and belonging in the classroom coupled with a bend toward perfectionism and an overall fear of failure and the labeling of such made it difficult to be in that space. As a result, much of my schooling was marred by failure, reclassification, and isolation. The fact that I graduated at all is really miraculous—the credit due to one high school counselor who made personal calls to my home. This wound lingers. I realize now the tre-mendous shame and guilt following me even to this day. However, it was not until I began to dig into and reflect on the feelings that were emerging for me as a teacher that I realized that this trauma still lingered and was exacerbated by the current dilemma.

It was, and remains, no small thing to reconcile all the parts of my-self. But the naming, and the acceptance of this story as my own, frac-tured the teaching identity I had cultivated to hide from this narrative. Acknowledging these truths allowed me to see how the work I was already doing was in response to this (for better or worse). This acknowledgement brought me to the realization that some failures lie in the system and not in myself. And, most importantly, I began to know that *this* way can't be the *only* way.

Preparing myself to return after winter break, I began embracing these struggles and patterns of myself and considering how I found joy in the midst of all of it. In this, I was inspired by the work of Ross Gay who, in a book reading for Gramercy Books, described the studying and seeking of joy as an "ethical imperative" and one as deserving of study and investigation as any other pursuit (Gramercy Books, 2020). What strikes me about Gay's notion is the idea of the work of joy. That joy is not simply given or found. It takes and is part of the work. This separates it from some of the social-emotional learning (SEL) and work we have been spoon-fed in professional development (PD) recently (Simmons, 2021). This joy-seeking work, instead, acknowledges that the road is hard, that there are barriers and trauma, but that hope remains. As I began to heal myself with this concept, I could see how it might be applied to the classroom as well.

A NOTE ON WHAT FOLLOWS

Reflecting on my own healing, I felt three concepts were key and reproducible in the classroom: community, visibility, and agency. I present here a brief discussion of some of the work my students and I immersed ourselves in. Although I am proud of the work we did, I am aware of how often products, with ideas of productivity and rigor, stand as the only lens in which we frame successful teaching and learning. I am also aware that an overt focus on these can obscure the fact that classrooms also need to be a space of joy—and how much of that depends not on products, but on presence. What is not illustrated here is the time spent just joking, talking about music, and the groups we formed just to spend time learning about one another. This work is equally important, but my hope is that by outlining these products here, I can illustrate not only the ways we made space for joy alongside learning but also the process involved in reflecting on and breaking from the current constructions of classrooms and schools.

RECONSIDERING BUSINESS AS USUAL: DECOLONIZING MY OWN PRACTICE

Schooling is, first and foremost, about control (Collins, 2021). Despite my own understanding of different modes of classroom management focused upon relationships (Campano, 2007) and my awareness of the policing of Black and Brown bodies in schools (Mallozzi, 2015), much of the classroom decisions I make (or do not make) are centered around a fear of the loss of control. Clearly, some degree of authority is necessary, and embedded, in teaching, but one of the major tensions I faced in moving towards a new curriculum comes from imagined ideas of where this authority is lost or gained.

In person, it is common practice to create seating charts to aid in classroom management. Also common is the practice of frequently rotating these seats, ensuring students do not get too talkative (read safe) with any one person. When I was faced with students who literally did not and would not know each other, I began to question this practice. As the year began, we developed what we called our "home" groups. That is the group we would frequently join during breakout rooms and small-group sessions. In this construction, I was hoping for the opposite of what I described earlier. Instead, the goal became for students to chat. We even developed a weekly practice of "good things" (borrowed from a friend and former member of *Teaching Out Loud*) where we shared a good thing going on or something we were looking forward to. In this practice, students were encouraged to, and some frequently did, go off topic. This grouping was essential for some students in finding new/any friendships. By the end of the year, we extended these kinds of groupings, allowing for other small-group meetings throughout the week.

As we returned from winter break in the 2020–2021 school year, I felt it was important for students to have discussions of self-care. Audre Lorde (1988) is credited with birthing the term "self-care." In her discussion of this practice, she stated, "Caring for myself is not self-indulgence, it is self-preservation, and that is an act of political warfare" (p. 130). Despite my earlier notions of school as a break from outside stressors, hxstorically that has not been the case. School spaces frequently tax, exhaust, and push out students, particularly those who are the most marginalized (Morris, 2018). In this new normal, this was doubly the case. In my mind, if we had any hope to come out of the gauntlet of the year, self-care was going to need to be part of the discussion. To frame this, I introduced students to our thematic question that I informed them we would be exploring the rest of the year: "How do people resist and persist toward joy?" We spent the remainder of the year considering this through all areas of study.

Self-care is not listed under any standard. I doubt you will find it labeled as "best practice" in any sort of teacher preparation program (I certainly did not). Yet it became essential in our study in the spring of 2021. In this inquiry. I found that in order to humanize the classroom, to move toward goals of visibility, community, and agency, I had to acknowledge the ways in which the classroom, myself, and school itself might be working in opposition to this. Some of the ways I confronted my practice are noted earlier. In addition, here are some other tensions that arose:

- With discussions of learning loss rampant (*All Things Considered*, 2021; Kang, 2022; Meckler & Natanson, 2020; Perea 2020) there was pressure nationally and locally to "fill the gaps" and focus on skills alone. My plan detailed later clearly did not do that, or at least not as a focus. Further, such a perspective centers school as the only place where learning occurs. A notion that disregards the multitude of learning that happens in our daily lives and experiences (Gonzalez et al., 2005). As the year carried on, it became important to me that we pushed back on this in the classroom. I wanted students to see themselves as knowledgeable about their own bodies and minds and to see value and wisdom in their outside-of-school actions and relationships.
- I am a writing-heavy teacher. In this, I believe in genre study and writing workshops as detailed by educators like Nancy Atwell (2014), Penny Kittle (2008), and Katie Wood Ray (2006). Due to the restrictions of online teaching, and honestly, just pure exhaustion, I had to not abandon these models but to extend them, pushing into digital composing and oral storytelling, which in turn expanded notions and expectations of literacy and writing in the classroom.
- Reading, too, was expanded. Without access to books (libraries were closed in the state, and leaving texts for students to pick up had mixed results), I was pushed to utilize resources from the library, like Hoopla. The platform prioritizes comics as a text. While these texts are worthy of study (Cornell-Boerman & Kim, 2020; McCloud, 1994), they are often viewed skeptically in classroom spaces. Thus, centering these kinds of texts as our primary novels was a step in a new direction.

TOWARD A PURSUIT OF JOY IN PEDAGOGY

Student and parent surveys I had sent out all throughout the first semester highlighted a continued need for student play. This was echoed by staff in a literal list of grievances that was served to administration at the end of the first semester of 2020–2021. In that list one comment stands out in particular, as a coworker stated that we [the school] "lost a sense of joy and fun in classrooms." They stated that when school reopens, we need to get back to that.

Students, too, tried to take this stance. I had noticed a push by students to this kind of play. Specifically, in my last class of the day, I was having a lot of difficulty with students clogging the chat in our Zoom meetings or blasting our Google Classroom page with conversation. As I journaled about this occurrence (and my annoyance with it), I began to view this "misbehavior" in a different light. Instead of work avoidance, I saw it also as what it was/is: play. Students knowledgeable and joy-seeking themselves were attempting to fit this missing interaction on their own.

As a result, we began to create a class Discord. (Discord is a chat app popular among the gaming community.) It allows for numerous forms of communication: phone calls, screen sharing, texting. In reality it functions pretty similarly to Google Classroom. The issue, however, is a perceived lack of control or oversight in the app, with many (including administration at my school) citing concerns about safety. I admit this was a concern of mine as well, as the prospect that I could not control what was posted (although I found out I could) and how and when individuals interact was alarming. But students thought otherwise. Through our student design meetings at lunch, students came and explained how Discord worked, brainstormed a code of conduct, and designed the virtual space itself. Throughout the semester, the Discord hosted a book club, gaming sessions, manga and anime suggestions, memes, and frequent posting of fits (outfits). All of this was driven and sustained by students.

IMAGINING NEW CURRICULUM

We started the new year with a discussion of what it has taken to even show up to class. We mapped out our own self-care strategies and set out to document them in video or photo. Afterwards, students created photo essays or digital stories. Each of these detailed and told the story of each individual's modes of self-care. Some students documented the numerous ways they stayed in contact with friends and families—virtual and in-person meetups, video games, lengthy phone calls; some documented the need to get out and be active—sports, geocaching, exercise. Many students also discussed the need to create: writing, crafting and Minecrafting, photography, drawing, painting, and music all featured prominently in their pieces. We returned to these pieces several times as we learned about revision by adding voiceover narration and reworking them. This was an idea I gathered from Cruz Medina in an NCTE presentation titled, "Rascuache Technology Pedagogy: Making Do with a Confluence of Resources" (Medina, 2021). Finally, we practiced our oratory skills as we presented our work to home groups (small groups we have met in at least once a week since the beginning of the school

Figure 7.1. Student slide, which shows some of the self-care practices they have adopted.

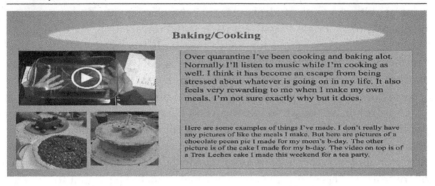

year) and reflected on the commonalities among us as we created a shared map of self-care and blogged about what we saw in each other's pieces (see Figure 7.1).

We also turned to literature. Due to the accessibility of it, we turned specifically to graphic novels. As we did, we thought about writing as a space to investigate hardship and considered the themes and lessons characters uncovered as we read the graphic novels *Flamer* by Mike Curato (2020), *Dragon Hoops* by Gene Luen Yang (2020), *Oracle Code* by Marieke Najikamp (2020), *Magic Fish* by Trung Lee Nguyen (2020), *March* by Andrew Aydin and John Lewis (2013), *New Kid* by Jerry Craft (2019), and *Hey, Kiddo* by Jarrett Krosocza (2018). What resulted was similar to the literature circles (Daniels & Stienke, 2004) in that students chose the novel they read. However, Zoom fatigue and difficulty scaffolding discussion prevented the traditional group meetings and discussion. Instead, we turned to our blogs. Through this mode, students reflected on the kinds of barriers characters faced in the novels. For example, the book *Flamer* by Mike Curato discusses the intersections of race and sexuality and how certain climates and cultures—in this case Boy Scouts—limit space for people who do not identify as White and/or heterosexual. After finishing the novels, students continued discussion through their blogs, analyzing characterization and conflict, and blogged the themes of the novels, specifically considering what authors might be telling us about our guiding question: How do these characters seek joy amidst turmoil?

Turning from novels, we thought deeply about the power of imagination and dreams, exploring speeches by Martin Luther King Jr., poems by Eve L. Ewing, photography by Dawoud Bey, and music by John Denver and hip hop group Arrested Development. From these creators we considered how folx had brought upon new realities by considering/dreaming new ways of doing or being. This discussion led to the creation of two pieces of curriculum investigating the concept of imagination.

First, we created memoir pieces about our own uses of imagination. Students discussed imaginary friends, unstructured games, and many other forms of play, but what was interesting was an effort by several to discuss the purpose behind such imagining. Some noted they "had no friends"; others noted a need of safety in imagination (several narratives—including my own—discussed how stuffed animals were seen as protectors in the nighttime).

Continuing our discussion of imagination and memoir, students also created fictionalized memoir as a form of counter-story. We read from Eve L. Ewing's "(Re)Telling" poem series from her book *Electric Arches* (2017) and then created our own (Re)Tellings. In them, students stood up to bullies, imagined loss differently, invented new family dynamics, and so forth.

Students also engaged in research. Students interviewed family members and/or other students in an attempt to again delve into our question of: "How do people persist and resist towards joy?" We then took these interviews and considered the theme of the research and made them into *Humans of New York*–inspired pieces, or, in one class, we showcased answers to this question by editing the interviews down into short 4- to 5-minute conversations inspired by Story Corps.

Lastly, we used our final to think about our future (see Figure 7.2). In this, I was deeply impacted by discussions of Afrofuturism during the Abolitionist Teaching Network (ATN) workshop entitled "Black Futures and Joy" on February 25, 2021 (Love et al., 2021) and the text *Freedom Dreaming* (2002) by Robin Kelley. After attending to this new knowledge, students and I engaged in a discussion of the word home. And after listening and looking closely at the music of hip hop group Arrested Development and John Denver, students developed a working definition for the word, denoting it as any place that features comfort, safety, relaxation, and allows you to be yourself. One student, in particular, noted that this may not even be an actual place, but instead a person or even an object.

In the culmination of our year together, we used this discussion as a springboard to create digital collages of "home." Students considered what objects would need to be in their home in order for it to be a place of joy. In this, students were required to consider not just their visions of the future but to display the texts, people, ideas, and self-care that would exist in such a space. The honors class, specifically, had to consider current barriers (systemic issues) and research and include movements working against this.

Figure 7.2. Student discussion of their vision of the future.

My dream future

My dream future would be a
place where the world is at
the perfect temperature and
natural disasters happen at
the right frequencies.
Everyone is equal and and
there is no military or police
because there would be no
reason to fight. Everyone
gets equal opportunities, and
girls and women can walk
down busy streets with out
being afraid.

IMPLICATIONS

*Community matters. Collectivity matters. . . . If we can't get along with each
other, and we can't take responsibility for what we do to each other, then what
the hell are we doing?*

—*Mariame Kaba* (2021, p. 171)

The pause in the status quo of schooling—whether it be the literal pause
due to COVID-19 or the threatened one as teachers organized in response
to pandemic working conditions (Gewertz, 2020)—provided an opportunity to see school in new ways. Bettina Love, in a web conference with
Haymarket Books (2020), echoed this, noting that because of the pandemic
"When we shut down schools . . . so much became possible." She continues
that standardized testing, lack of access to Internet or technology, things
that were considered the norm, were all done away with or addressed in
a matter of weeks. For me, too, this proved true. Without the ability to
carry on as normal, I was freed to expand my own notions. However, as we
returned to our classrooms in the late fall of 2021 it was clear this pause
was temporary. An overwhelming push to "return to normal" led my own

school to refuse to buy students items as simple as water bottles. It led to numerous schools shrugging their shoulders as teachers rang out about the impossibility of hybrid teaching. It led and will lead to a system that is violently inequitable. And I am tired. We should all be tired at this point, because what works for schools does not work for those within them, truly. Reflecting upon my narrative, it is clear the negative impact that status quo teaching has on everyone. Even those privileged in the system (myself a college graduate, sitting in a position of relative power) are not free.

* * *

So how do we get free? I don't have answers, but here is what I am left thinking about:

1. We can't work alone. At each turn in the pandemic year(s), I found myself reaching toward collaboration and collectivism. Whether it be conferences like NCTE, or Dismantling White Supremacy in Schools or groups like *Teaching Out Loud* or my co-conspirators in my specific space, I continually found myself seeking to work and learn with others. Ultimately, much of the work I am most proud of came from listening to and moving with others.
2. Schools need to tell the truth. I found most traction in my teaching when I was honest about my own hxstory of schooling and when I could be vulnerable enough to admit that I was unwell. The trauma I experienced as a young person still exists with me as an adult, and this is not due to a lack of internal work on my part, but because schools continue to be bound up in institutionalized racism and White supremacy (Collins, 2021). Yet teachers are encouraged to compartmentalize and run from identities that do not mesh with their professional persona (Alsup, 2005). This is not to say teachers should be living out their trauma within the classroom, but rather that teacher identity plays out whether we are aware of it or not. We need to be aware of these identities to be well for our students. And the same is true for our institutions. The trauma endured these past years, and to that point, the trauma endured in schools by folx since time immemorial, needs to be remembered and centered as we begin to imagine our way forward.

REFERENCES

All Things Considered. (2021, October 16). The pandemic has left many students months behind in school subjects. NPR. https://www.npr.org/programs/all-things-considered/2021/10/16/1046779457/all-things-considered-for-october-16-202

Alsup, J. (2005). *Teacher identity discourses: Negotiating personal and professional spaces*. Routledge.

Atwell, N. (2014). *In the middle: A lifetime of learning about writing, reading, and adolescents*. Heinemann.

Campano, G. (2007). *Immigrant students and literacy: Reading, writing, and remembering*. Teachers College Press.

Cohen, J. (2020, July 14). A teenager didn't do her online schoolwork. So a judge sent her to juvenile detention. Propublica. https://www.propublica.org/article/a-teenager-didnt-do-her-online-schoolwork-so-a-judge-sent-her-to-juvenile-detention

Collins, C. (2021). It was always about control. Learning for Justice. https://www.learningforjustice.org/magazine/spring-2021/it-was-always-about-control

Cornell-Boerman, W., & Kim, J. (2020). *Using graphic novels in the English language arts classroom*. Bloomsbury Academic.

Craft, J. (2019). *New kid*. Quill Tree Books.

Curato, M. (2020). *Flamer*. Henry Holt and Co.

Daniels, H., & Seineken, N. (2004). *Mini-lessons for literature circles*. Heinemann.

Dutro, E. (2019). *The vulnerable heart of literacy: Centering trauma as powerful pedagogy*. Teachers College Press.

Elahi, A. (2020, May 13). Sleeping while Black: Louisville police kill unarmed Black woman. NPR. https://www.npr.org/2020/05/13/855705278/sleeping-while-black-louisville-police-kill-unarmed-black-woman

Elfrink, T. (2020, September 25). A teacher saw a BB gun in a 9-year-old's room during online class. He faced expulsion. *The Washington Post*. https://www.washingtonpost.com/nation/2020/09/25/louisiana-student-bbgun-expulsion/

Ewing, E. L. (2017). *Electric arches*. Haymarket Books.

Gewertz, C. (2020, August 20). New York city teachers' union threatens strike over school reopenings. *Education Week*. https://www.edweek.org/teaching-learning/new-york-city-teachers-union-threatens-strike-over-school-reopenings/2020/08

González, N., Moll, L. C., & Amanti, C. (2005). *Funds of knowledge: Theorizing practice in households, communities, and classrooms*. Routledge.

Gramercy Books. (2020, February 3). Ross Gay, poet and author of "The Book of Delights," in conversation with Hanif Abdurraqib. YouTube. https://www.youtube.com/watch?v=uRKCtC08sVo

Grzeszczak, J. (2020, September 4). Two Colorado students suspended from school after handling toy guns during virtual classes. *Newsweek*. https://www.newsweek.com/two-colorado-students-suspended-school-after-handling-toy-guns-during-virtual-classes-1529764

Haymarket Books. (2020, June 23). Abolitionist teaching and the future of our schools. YouTube. https://www.youtube.com/watch?v=uJZ3RPJ2rNc&t=3557s

hooks, b. (1994). *Teaching to transgress: Education as the practice of freedom*. Routledge.

Hsieh, B. (2016). Professional identity development as a framework in working with preservice secondary teacher candidates. *Teacher Education Quarterly, 43*(2), 93–112.

Kaba, M. (2021). *We do this 'til we free us*. Haymarket Books.

Kang, J. C. (2022, January 10). Our kids are behind in school. Here's how to help them. *The New York Times.* https://www.nytimes.com/2022/01/10/opinion/covid-school-closures.html

Kelley, R. (2002). *Freedom dreaming: The Black radical imagination.* Beacon Press.

Kittle, P. (2008). *Write beside them: Risk, voice, and clarity in high school writing.* Heinemann.

Krosocza, J. (2018) *Hey, kiddo.* Graphix.

Land, K. (2020, October 2). Far too many NM students are 'in the wind.' *The Albuquerque Journal.* https://www.abqjournal.com/1502811/far-too-many-nm-students-are-in-the-wind-ex-distance-learning-taking-a-social-emotional-and-educational-toll-on-families.html

Lewis, J., & Aydin, A. (2013). *March: Book one.* Top Shelf Productions.

Lorde, A. (1988). *A burst of light.* Firebrand Books.

Love, B. L. (2019). *We want to do more than survive: Abolitionist teaching and the pursuit of educational freedom.* Beacon Press.

Love, B. L., Robinson, S. M, G., & Sealey-Ruiz, Y. (2021, February 25). Black Futures and Black Joy [Virtual Workshop]. *Abolitionist Teaching Network.*

Mallozzi, C. A. (2015). Disciplined within a discipline: English teachers are bound to be human bodies. In G. Enriquez, E. Johhnson, S. Kontourvaki, & C. A. Mallozzi (Eds.) *Literacies, learning and the body: Putting theory and research into pedagogical practice* (pp. 57–71). Routledge.

McCloud, S. (1994). *Understanding comics.* HarperCollins Publishers.

Meckler, L., & Natanson, H. (2020, December 6) 'A lost generation': Surge of research reveals students sliding backward, most vulnerable worst affected. *The Washington Post.* https://www.washingtonpost.com/education/students-falling-behind/2020/12/06/88d7157a-3665-11eb-8d38-6aea1adb3839_story.html

Medina, C. (2021, November 19). Rascuache Technology Pedagogy: Making do with a confluence of resources [Conference Presentation]. NCTE 2020 Convention.

Morris, M. (2018). *Pushout: The criminalization of black girls in schools.* The New Press.

Nguyen, T. L. (2020). *The magic fish.* Random House Graphic.

Nijkamp, M. (2020). *Oracle code.* DC Comics.

Ortiz, K. (2020, December 1). Guest column: Teachers are heroes, facing adversity through a pandemic. *The Albuquerque Journal.* https://www.abqjournal.com/1521658/guest-column-teachers-are-heroes-facing-adversity-through-a-pandemic.html

Perea, S. (2020, October 28). NM students face learning loss. *The Albuquerque Journal.* https://www.abqjournal.com/1512119/nm-students-face-learning-loss.html

Ray Wood, K. (2006). *Study driven: A framework for planning units of study in the writing workshop.* Heinemann.

Richter, F. (2021, February, 4). COVID-19 has caused a huge amount of lost working hours. Weforum. https://www.weforum.org/agenda/2021/02/covid-employment-global-job-loss/

Robbins, A. (2020, March 20). Teachers deserve more respect. *The New York Times.* https://www.nytimes.com/2020/03/20/opinion/sunday/teachers-coronavirus.html

Simmons, D. (2021). Why SEL alone isn't enough. *Educational Leadership*. *78*(6), 30–34.

Thompson, C. (2020, December 6). Schools confront 'off the rails' numbers of failing grades. *The Albuquerque Journal*. https://www.abqjournal.com/1524123/schools-confront-off-the-rails-numbers-of-failing-rades.html

Williams, B. (2020, May 28). George Floyd is not the first black man to die in Minneapolis police custody. NPR. https://www.npr.org/2020/05/28/863605594/george-floyd-is-not-the-first-black-man-to-die-in-minneapolis-police-custody

Williams, P. J. (1991). *The alchemy of race and rights*. Harvard University Press.

Yang, G. L. (2020). *Dragon hoops*. First Second.

CHAPTER 8

Self-Care

A Radical Space for Growth, Equity, and the Rehumanization of Educators

Damon R. Carbajal

> Caring for myself is not self-indulgence, it is self-preservation, and that is an act of political warfare.
>
> —Audre Lorde

TEACHER CARE VERSUS TEACHER SELF-CARE

It is a warm spring New Mexico day in May 2019, and my *Teaching Out Loud* colleagues are meeting for the final time before the summer break. We are in a local coffee shop surrounded by the buzz of people and joy in the air as the end of the school year fast approaches. The table we sit at and the people who create our immediate *Teaching Out Loud* familia offer a space of safety and *resolana* that feels separate from the action at the coffee shop. In this space, we have three preservice teachers who are finishing up their student teaching, two veteran teachers, and the leader of the group, a professor of education at the local university. We have all grown into one unit as the year has continued, learning and growing into understanding each other. As we go around the table, we dive into basic hellos and check-ins, all with the common thread of the stresses of life, teaching, and the struggle for balance. We each are candid with how we feel, and there are large variations in the feelings of the group members as a collective. There is the general aura of exhaustion and the anticipation of a much-needed break from teaching.

Amid the general welcome and check-in, we discuss a darker side of teaching that is driven by negative stress and the often-unnoted desire of being a martyr teacher: "The notion of the superhero or 'martyr' teacher who single-handedly, tirelessly, and miraculously transforms an entire group of students—to the detriment of his or her health, personal life, and well-being" (Hill, 2018). As a student teacher, this idea is what we are held to. We are taught all about best practice, what good classroom management is, how one should and should not do things, how one's classroom should look, what one should do to prepare for a job, and the list goes on and on, but rarely do we ask the question, if at all, of "How are you?" A question that is simple yet warrants false answers. When someone asks me *how I am*, I usually use the canned answer of "busy and tired, but good." Nine times out of 10, that is a lie, not being tired or busy, but that I am "good." We are conditioned to say things like this to save face and to show that we are okay and to not show weakness. This occurs frequently in teaching because we often feel that we cannot show weakness. After all, we will not be taken seriously, students will overrun us, and we will never get a job. Thus, we pretend we are okay.

The moment that broke this barrier was when one of my colleagues was vastly honest with how she was doing; she was not okay, and she showed it. This could not occur in traditional professional development, but it was possible due to the bond that was formed as a *Teaching Out Loud* community of educators. To openly break down and cry in a group setting shows vulnerability. It takes courage and trust in those around you. They shared that they were failing at teaching and scared that they would not be successful. It was a moment of bravery that was followed by support *for* an educator *by* educators. Support at that moment was not only important but critical for the growth of the colleague, as well as allowing them space to show their true emotions. After the outburst of emotion, headed by the veteran teachers in the space, was a conversation about the truth of being an educator in a broken system. We each must take everything with a grain of salt because nothing we do will ever be good enough for the outside eye. No one is perfect, and no teacher should feel that they must be perfect because that is never the case. At that moment, I was taken aback but realized the *resolana* that was created through the space where we can put down our mask of being the model teacher, the model student, and the model person and be real with who we are, what our struggles are, and how we are all human at the core.

After reflecting on this moment, I noted my project for the year, "You Will Be Found: An Exploration of Mental Health in the English Language Arts Classroom," focused on mental health and suicidality among youth as told via the musical *Dear Evan Hansen* (Levenson et al., 2017) and related materials. The project used the musical as the anchor text to teach about argumentative writing, with a focus on situating the lived realities of mental health and suicidality faced by many youth throughout New Mexico. The unit was centered around these topics, but was deeply enriched with writing of all genres, practicing public speaking skills, and most importantly a focus on the need to heal from past and current traumas. The project used a variety of self-care techniques embedded in the lesson to allow students a space to vent, grow, and hopefully heal from their past and current mental health traumas.

Thus, I noted that, in general, our society lacked self-care for educators by educators. In this moment of reflection, I realized that I was not practicing what I taught, and this was a symptom of what it meant to be a teacher as told by a teacher preparation program and society overall. During my tenure in a teacher preparation program, there was the unspoken focus on making everything perfect (i.e., a 15-page lesson plan for one class period, a teaching autobiography that discloses all your trauma and is scored on grammar and not content, and the list goes on and on). So, there was a push to be a perfect teacher and do everything even if it came at your own cost of well-being. For example, one of the requirements for the final teaching seminar course was a stewardship project where preservice educators were supposed to work in and with the community to create something. When this project was explained in the class, it was described as something groundbreaking that should push us. So, my peers and I wrote a grant and put on a student community showcase because that was what I thought I had to do. When in all reality most of my peers tutored for an hour or two a week and did not create a huge event. I am grateful that the students were able to experience the event, but it came at a large cost to my mental health and overall well-being. There is something powerful about being in a space where you can be your holistic self and share similar struggles to a group of people that understand the struggles. Recognizing the absence of this kind of intentional space, I posed the question: What does self-care *for* educators, *by* educators, look like and how can this be done effectively in a variety of mediums? This story comes before the COVID-19 pandemic, and the latter part of this question originated with moving from in-person work to virtual work and the tensions that emerged as a result.

SITUATING EDUCATOR MENTAL HEALTH IN THE CURRENT CLIMATE

The need for self-care has never been higher, especially for educators and students as they have been living in the virtual universe for more than a year. Being on a screen all day has led to high levels of fatigue caused by screens (aka Zoom fatigue) (Sklar, 2020). Screen fatigue and the strain of being on a screen all day are mentally and physically exhausting, but to learn and teach during the pandemic, one had to log in daily for many hours. When screen fatigue is multiplied by everyday life being virtual, it is easy to understand how we have moved beyond fatigue and into exhaustion. Not only is this state unhealthy, but it is not conducive to learning and teaching. This exhaustion is compounded by the stress of the world (i.e., a global pandemic, a presidential election, racial tensions) and the lack of human interaction, which gave way to higher rates of suicide ideation, suicide attempts, and suicide overall (New Mexico Department of Health, 2021). Connection is a basic human need, and thus, we need this to be met, but the pandemic has made it very hard to do so.

While there has been a substantial outcry about student mental health, which is warranted as the lack of socialization and safety that school provides has been missing for a year, educator mental health has been neglected. Educator mental health is something that has been neglected forever, but the pandemic has heightened the lack of care for educators. We see this with the high levels of "burnout" among veteran educators. According to Schroeder (2020), "Too often we use the term 'burnout' loosely. Yet it is a defined condition." Burnout can best be defined as ". . . emotional exhaustion, cynicism and ineffectiveness in the workplace, and by chronic negative responses to stressful workplace conditions. While not considered a mental illness, burnout can be considered a mental health issue" (Mathieu & Baynton, 2022). This is the daily experience for educators and has only been exacerbated by the pandemic, where they have been forced to balance many things and uphold the notion of being a flawless teacher. This pressure has taken a toll. For example, "among the poll respondents, 55 percent of veteran teachers with more than 30 years of experience said they were now considering leaving the profession. So did 20 percent of teachers with less than 10 years' experience" (Singer, 2020). These are highly alarming rates that are going to add to the educator shortage in the United States. So, besides the fact that educators need to be able to have positive mental health, we need to make changes now, so we are not dealing with the repercussions later that will ultimately negatively affect teachers, educators, students, and the future overall.

INTERSECTIONALITY OF A QUEER CHICANX EDUCATOR

For true intersectional work to be understood, one must note the author's positionality and social locations as it influences their lens and their position within the specific work and the larger context. I am originally from Las Cruces, New Mexico, where the majority of my family resides and has resided for many years. We are a family that the border crossed several times, and we ended up on the United States' side of the U.S.-Mexico border. I am mestiza and define myself as a *Mexicano mutt*. My father is Mexican, and my mother is White. This has led me to identify and be identified as a White Mexican. This social location grants me privilege, as I am White-passing in many spaces, which I acknowledge and understand plays into how I am treated by others around me. In addition to my racial and ethnic social location, I am also a gay, queer, cisgender male. This intersectional social location has been one of the primary stressors as I move through life. I am an effeminate man in looks, mannerisms, and tone of voice, as well as other factors. This effeminity has shaped my understanding of the world, as it puts me in a position where hegemonic masculinity and machismo have othered my being. Also, I am heavy-set, struggle with the invisible dis/abilities of anxiety and depression, and come from a location where I experienced past trauma that involved physical and verbal bullying, sexual assault, and bias due to low socioeconomic status. These factors have heavily influenced my outlook and perspectives, which is critical to note, as they have shaped this research project.

INQUIRY APPROACHES PRE- AND POST-COVID-19

The inquiry approach that was utilized for the exploration of self-care spaces for educators was based largely on an intersectional *theory in the flesh* (Moraga & Anzaldúa, 1981). In this sense, I intentionally created spaces where hands-on activities were situated in a way that could aid in combating the daily stress of teaching. The most effective way to do this was through piloting in-person workshops and, when the pandemic hit, to create a virtual online platform. This twofold approach was a 2-year inquiry process where the first year involved the in-person workshops series and the second year used the virtual online platform. With the New Mexico focus, the spaces were based on intersectional social-justice principles where Black, Indigenous, People of Color (BIPOC), queer, femme, and other marginalized voices were centered. We can liken the work to a live curriculum lab—just as a K–12 classroom is a living and breathing entity, the in-person workshop spaces and the virtual space act in the same manner. With this larger framework set, I will detail what the spaces and inquiry looked like in a pre–COVID-19 (Year 1: Fall 2019 to Spring 2020) and a COVID-19 world (Year 2: Fall 2020 to Spring 2021).

PRE-COVID-19 INQUIRY (YEAR 1: FALL 2019 TO SPRING 2020)

As I ended the first year of *Teaching Out Loud* in the spring of 2019 and had just finished my student teaching practicum, I began thinking about what my next *Teaching Out Loud* inquiry project would be. I was exhausted, and it struck me that as educators we were and are lacking concrete approaches to self-care. I began planning a workshop series for the fall semester. This epiphany occurred when reviewing the content from the previous year of teaching where I was looking at the implications of the *Dear Evan Hansen* unit, where mental health was centered for students and realized that educators were in need of similar self-care spaces but were not provided these spaces due to the constraints of the current education system. The workshop series I imagined, planned, and fine-tuned included three evening workshop sessions that focused on various entities of self-care and outlets for self-care. The three sessions that were put on during fall 2019 were (1) Writing as Therapy, (2) Art as Healing, and (3) Drama and Movement as Renewal. Each session lasted 90 minutes, occurred in a College of Education classroom (see Figure 8.1) at a local university, and was in the evening, a space that was not akin to a K–12 classroom, but a space that was a classroom in itself. Each session began with breaking bread and getting to know one another before delving into the hands-on activities and concluding with self and community reflection. The curriculum lab was physical and in-person. Workshops were created where educators gathered to heal and practice self-care for their holistic selves. To aid in promoting the self-care journey for the attending educators, the workshop sessions were broken down into four major parts: (1) time to enter the space and

Figure 8.1. In-person workshop setup for educator self-care workshop series.

gather food informally; (2) breaking the tension (introductions and breaking bread together); (3) workshop activities; and (4) closing (bringing the community collectively to a close).

This outlines the basic structure of the workshops but was adapted at each workshop session to fit the needs of the educators who attended and the level of comfort they had with the space. Overall, the inquiry was approached from a humanistic perspective with a focus on educator need, desire, and opportunity for growth. For example, activities included creating scenes based on a name we had been called in the past, painting using masking tape, and enacting various self-reflective writing prompts with a variety of materials. I wanted to ensure that there was an activity or session in the workshop series that allowed for all educators to take something away (i.e., a letter to themselves for a bad day, a piece of art they could hang on the wall, a written scene to read and reflect upon). To accomplish this, a variety of multimodalities were used, including writing, drawing, painting, drama games, conversation, and self/group-reflection. By using the variety of multimodalities and varied activities, I noted that the educators in the space had a sense of release, as they may not have felt one activity was helpful, but there was something that they latched onto and enjoyed. This was made clear during the postworkshop survey with comments such as, "I really enjoyed the letter exercise—it's a great way to reflect on the good about yourself"; "I had never made an emotion painting before, I enjoyed it"; and "I liked the vocal tongue twisters." Also, by providing activities that could be accomplished by all and help break the ice, it gave the educators a sense of security. For example, starting the Art as Healing workshop, I had participants draw with their eyes closed. All the drawings were a mix of technicolor, and they all were similar, thus it broke down the idea that one is "not a good artist" because even the best artist would end up with a similar style of work at the end of the activity. This was just one of many activities, but this illuminates the style of the sessions. In addition to this, the workshops acted as a sampling of many activities that educators could use on their own and provided various levels of time commitment. For example, they could do a simple drawing activity for 3–5 minutes or engage in extended self-reflective writing for a longer time period. This setup was chosen to ensure that all educators could connect their identities and time to self-care for themselves.

An intersectional self-care framework was utilized where the activities were modeled after frameworks from the BIPOC community, with an emphasis on Chicanx models. I was heavily influenced by the notion of creating a space of *resolana*. This space led to more concrete data sets (i.e., the curriculum that was created for the workshops, photos from the workshop, and the pieces created in the workshop by the participants). This data was coupled with more concrete ideas with surveys from participants, facilitator reflections, and testimonios of truth told via each participant following the workshops (i.e., informal conversations, messages shared).

COVID-19 INQUIRY (YEAR 2: FALL 2020 TO SPRING 2021)

Following the conclusion of the first set of workshops, the COVID-19 pandemic hit the world hard, and all in-person events were halted overnight. This occurred in the middle of March 2020 and caused the summer workshop planning to be halted, as the future was highly uncertain and educators were pushed into virtual learning hell with little to no time for adjusting to change. The pandemic caused a shift for me, and the inquiry was placed on hold while I was navigating a whole new world of being a graduate student, community educator, graduate assistant, employee, researcher, and community leader. This new learning and the forced transition occurred until the middle of the fall 2020 semester due to a variety of factors at which point the need for educator self-care was beyond overdue, and I was left with the sentiment that I needed to do something, but what I could do was a burning question. I reflected on my mental health journey and the *Dear Evan Hansen* unit. This was manifested and taught because of my past and my aim at helping students create a brighter future, and this is where I started. Recognizing the value of in-person engagement, I was left with the question: How can educator self-care occur in a pandemic, and what is the most productive way in which to foster it, especially in light of Zoom fatigue? Thus, I opted to create a virtual self-care space that was housed via Facebook and consisted of sharing videos, resources, quotes, and self-care tips. I knew the world was "Zoomed" and screened out; thus, holding workshops virtually was not aiding in self-care and doing the exact opposite. For example, an educator may have logged into the virtual workshop session to enact self-care to heal, but because it was on a screen, it could have backfired, and they ended up leaving the space more tired and fatigued than when they logged on, whereas they may have healed more through simply taking a break from digital spaces. Thus, the Facebook page Intersectional Self-Care (@xselfcare) was born out of the desire to provide small bits of self-care while scrolling on a phone (as most folx do with social media). One may note that social media spaces can be hostile to self-care, but I argue back against that notion. Yes, we must acknowledge the fact that social media can be a highly contentious space, thus that is why I decided to create a Facebook group where only I could post as an administrator. This provided a space of safety within the confines of social media and allowed for folx who were on their main feeds to be exposed to the page via random posts being mixed in with the regular feed. I view @xselfcare as a space of *resolana*, or a space of political action within a larger system, within the larger world of social media (Montiel et al., 2009)—a political space that was created out of the need to move from survival to thriving. The types of media that were posted to the Facebook page were a mix of self-care tips; videos to enact self-care practices; community events that were intersectional and/or self-care in nature; and quotes from varied intersectional peoples attesting to self-care, resilience, and thriving and not simply surviving. This was a new kind of inquiry and one that felt very distant—outside of posting items and people interacting with posts via likes and comments, the human nature of the work was missing. This has led to a new kind of data that is highly quantitative and based solely on numbers and is outside of my usual qualitative work.

As a response to my graduate work, self-growth, and the acts of racism that were illuminated via riots over the summer of 2020 and continue into today (Abrams, 2021), I wanted to create intersectional self-care via a digital platform, just as I had done before with the in-person workshops, but this time it was even more essential. The focus on BIPOC, queer, femme, and other marginalized communities was essential, and that is why Intersectional Self-Care was created—it is a space for all, but a space that centers on those from the most marginalized communities. In its first iteration (Year 1: workshop series), the inquiry focused largely on self-care that was unintentionally rooted in White paradigms and ideologies. Through the events of the outside world (BLM, *Yazzie Martinez v. State of New Mexico*, etc.) and my growth working on a master's degree in Chicanx studies and graduate certificate in "Race" and Social Justice, I realized the foundations of the Year 1 workshop series. In that moment, I knew I needed to be more international with creating self-care that was not rooted in White supremacist ideologies but rooted in marginalized communities and work to actively center on these lost voices. To make this possible, I flipped my focus to center on work and words of those from marginalized communities. This has occurred through sharing the content and ensuring that we, as a virtual space, are centering on BIPOC, queer, and other marginalized voices. This was done by posting content that was intersectional in nature (i.e., quotes from non-White, non-cisgender peoples, sharing articles and videos that highlighted specific paradigms of nonmainstream theories, and uplifting images that aided in breaking the stereotypes surrounding marginalized communities). I took this approach to provide space for educators who come from marginalized communities but also to highlight that self-care is for all and does not require money or other resources. This notion relies on the fact that the educator has an Internet-accessed device, but during a pandemic, options are limited to safe access. This, in turn, aids in highlighting the many issues with the capitalistic society of the United States where pandemic teaching and learning became more accessible to those with resources.

CAUTIONS, TAKEAWAYS, AND A RADICAL FUTURE OF SELF-CARE

The heart of this inquiry and my work overall focus on creating and maintaining spaces where equity, healing, and truth can occur for all communities. The only way for this holistic healing to occur is through centering mental health through self-care. I also caution that self-care is not monolithic, but varies from person to person; thus, we need to acknowledge that the spaces noted earlier may not align with one's personal vision of self-care, and this represents one of the key tensions with self-care work overall. We (society) try to boil down self-care into one thing when in reality there is no self-care with a capital "s." This is a trap that extends into the stigma associated with mental health. It can be easy to assume, for example, that commodified versions of self-care like spa trips are what educators need, when, in reality, self-care differs from person to person and can include a multitude of things such as engaging politically and taking public stances against issues of racism and hate. Educators are humans, not martyrs for the common good; they need to enact mental well-being like every human that walks this planet. Moreover, like all humans, how they care for themselves will vary from person to person and should not be essentialized.

With this rehumanizing radical stance at the forefront, we need to examine how we can achieve a more individualized, less commodified, and more sustainable version of self-care that allows educators the healing spaces they need. As my inquiry attests, healing did not occur via a digital space and was more likely to occur in the in-person workshop spaces. Thus, my research suggests that healing spaces can be more effective in person. But this also calls into question how schools should proceed best with enacting self-care. For example, a tension persisted in the in-person workshops series (Year 1) when workshops were held in the classroom space, which was not always conducive to deep reflection and radical self-care. This also indicates that the notion of self-care cannot be a mandated aspect of education—it needs to occur organically in a space of comfort and at the discretion of the educator. This does not mean that schools and districts should not aid in providing spaces and opportunities for self-care, but these spaces should be created by and for educators without mandating attendance or expecting immediate buy-in. As the state reopens, collective, organic, in-person educator self-care can become a reality, but we must continue to note that self-care looks different for all.

These learnings and tensions lead me to contemplate the following questions: What will the long-term effects of the pandemic be on educators, students, and community mental health? I also wonder how I can bridge in-person self-care workshops with the online social media platform to allow more access and opportunities for self-care in an authentic way. And lastly, I wonder how schools will adapt to getting back into the classroom. Will there be a shift to "normal" and will we forget the importance of mental health altogether?

As an educator, scholar, and activist, I want to reiterate that this account is not meant to highlight the struggles of educators in order to evoke pity, but to highlight the need to view educators as human. The inquiry and the pandemic aided in revealing the truth behind the rose-colored glasses of education and what it truly means to be an educator. Thus, as an educator I want you to leave those rose-colored glasses on the floor and not fall back into the trap that everything will be okay once the pandemic ends. The education system is broken, and currently the future of our country lies on the broken backs of educators who can only heal by being viewed as human. We, as a society, must create change for the future because educators are the backbone of the future, and they deserve better than what they deal with today. Connecting this back to the narrative we started with, all educators need to have a space where they can be their true authentic self and work through the emotional toll that teaching takes, and *Teaching Out Loud* is a unique space that allows this. We need more spaces like *Teaching Out Loud*. We need spaces where all educators can express themselves and be supported. Sadly, the current landscape often renders these approaches impossible. My trajectory as an educator, scholar, and activist aims at making this a reality, but it is something that cannot be done alone. As I end this reflection on a lifelong inquiry, I leave you with a call to action; no matter what space you occupy, what position you hold, or who you are, you need to uplift the voices of educators and push for their rehumanization. One of the most critical ways to do this is to provide spaces for them to be human, enact self-care that works for them, and be an educator accomplice and not just an ally (Love, 2019).

REFERENCES

Abrams, Z. (2021, April 9). The mental health impact of anti-Asian racism. American Psychological Association, *52*(5), 22. https://www.apa.org/monitor/2021/07/impact-anti-asian-racism

Hill, N. (2018, July 25). Teachers, we don't have to be martyrs. *Education Week*. https://www.edweek.org/teaching-learning/opinion-teachers-we-dont-have-to-be-martyrs/2018/07

Levenson, S., Pasek, B., & Paul, J. (2017). *Dear Evan Hansen*. Theatre Communication Group.

Love, B. L. (2019). *We want to do more than survive: Abolitionist teaching and the pursuit of educational freedom*. Beacon Press.

Mathieu, F., & Baynton, M. A. (2022, June 16). Burnout response for leaders. Workplace Strategies for Mental Health. https://www.workplacestrategies formentalhealth.com/resources/burnout-response-for-leaders

Montiel, M., Atencio, T., & Mares, E. A. (2009). *Resolana: Emerging Chicano dialogues on community and globalization.* University of Arizona Press.

Moraga, C., & Anzaldúa, G. (1981). *This bridge called my back: Writings by radical women of color.* Persephone Press.

New Mexico Department of Health. (2021, December 6). New Mexico suicide deaths increase in 2020. New Mexico Department of Health. https://www.nmhealth.org/news/information/2021/12/?view=1739

Schroeder, R. (2020, December 11). Mental health epidemic: Dark shadow of the COVID pandemic. Inside Higher Ed. https://www.insidehighered.com/digital-learning/blogs/online-trending-now/mental-health-epidemic-dark-shadow-covid-pandemic

Singer, N. (2020, November 30). Teaching in the pandemic: 'This is not sustainable.' *The New York Times.* https://www.nytimes.com/2020/11/30/us/teachers-remote-learning-burnout.html

Sklar, J. (2020, April 24). 'Zoom fatigue' is taxing the brain. Here's why that happens. *National Geographic.* https://www.nationalgeographic.com/science/article/coronavirus-zoom-fatigue-is-taxing-the-brain-here-is-why-that-happens

Part III

CONCEPTUALIZING KEY TENETS OF CRITICAL TEACHER INQUIRY

CHAPTER 9

Moving Forward
Conceptual Tools and Promising Pedagogies for Teacher Inquiry and Practice

Katherine Crawford-Garrett and Kahlil Simpson

Teaching Out Loud was created in a post-2016 political climate shaped by hate speech, draconian immigration policies, political polarization, and pervasive fear and uncertainty. As we considered how to teach in contentious times, *Teaching Out Loud* transformed into a space that allowed us as educators to reimagine our practice within and against the dominant paradigms of professional development and a sociopolitical context that felt increasingly authoritarian.

Our work was intentionally based on three key tenets: intergenerationality, participatory processes, and public dissemination. While membership and social conditions changed and evolved, the group stayed committed to these principles.

Intergenerationality refers to the ways in which teachers interacted across the spectrum of experience as our group included preservice teachers, experienced educators, community educators, retired teachers, and university professors. Although preservice teachers appreciated the advice offered by the more experienced members, support was multifaceted and seldom unidirectional as we both examined and unpacked what it means to teach for equity across a diverse and complex set of educational contexts. Occasionally, these interactions played out in predictable ways, like when a less experienced educator needed support implementing bilingual literature circles in her classroom and the more experienced teachers in the group stepped in with concrete suggestions and ideas. However, the experienced educators also embraced vulnerability by sharing student work, lesson plans, classroom artifacts, and other elements that revealed the uncertainty we all share as educators. In doing so, less experienced teachers were able to offer perspectives that were often fresh and unique, as they had not been influenced or shaped by years within institutions or the public school system. This intergenerational exploration fostered trust and was free of judgment, allowing group members to grow as educators in their unique contexts.

Our group was also predicated upon and dedicated to a set of participatory processes that spanned both teaching and research. From using personal and professional check-ins to reading and discussing critical texts to engaging in the joint analysis of our teaching artifacts, our shared vulnerability grew over space and time and enabled us to deepen our commitment to each other and our individual and shared practices. For example, while our check-ins started off as a perfunctory approach to seeing how we were feeling and doing, these evolved over time to become an essential part of how we validated one another's humanity. For many of us, *Teaching Out Loud* was the only space we belonged to where we could interweave the personal, political, and professional aspects of our lives. This often meant tapping into the trauma that we experienced as students, naming these instances, and examining how they impacted our decisions and approaches to classroom teaching. For some of us, these traumas included the erasure of our identities; learning a whitewashed, Eurocentric, patriarchal curriculum; or being subjected to disciplinary practices when our bodies or minds did not conform to the image of an ideal student.

Our participatory processes were also essential to our research endeavors as we sought to document and publish the work of our group. While data was collected by Katy as the group facilitator, we engaged collaboratively in the analysis and writing process, including coding large volumes of data, identifying themes, and writing results for academic journals. Adding this layer of participation supported the overall ethos of the group—that it was a space where knowledge was developed collectively and where teachers could engage in important sense-making together.

The final tenet of our group was a commitment to public dissemination, which is not only central to our mission but also indexed by our name—*Teaching Out Loud*. We urged one another to share our work in our respective schools, community spaces, and other public arenas where the work would be seen and discussed by wider audiences. For example, Amanda's project included an art installation at a local library (see Figure 6.3) where students, families, and community members (and a district school board representative) could interact with students as they discussed their artistic interpretations. Damon's project involved having students create posters that were then placed throughout the school with the explicit aim of cultivating awareness around mental health. Kahlil hosted a poetry night that allowed students to showcase their engagement with critical topics through poetry to families, other students, and administrators. And stemming from this, students from the class also established a school poetry club, participated in a citywide slam, and—in 2021–2022—designed and developed a zine of art and poetry for distribution in the surrounding community.

In addition to the tenets noted earlier that were intentionally developed by the founders and members of *Teaching Out Loud*, other common threads unite our efforts and, specifically, this collection. First, across our 3 years together we noted the need for social and emotional learning to take on new forms, especially in postpandemic classrooms where students are struggling to (re)build relationships with their teachers and each other. While social and emotional learning was the espoused inquiry topic of only one member, in almost every project, social-emotional learning emerged as an urgent and salient topic as teachers wrestled with student responses to the pandemic, teaching and learning over Zoom, and increased economic precarity that afflicted Albuquerque and New Mexico during this time.

Embedded within their call for increased attention to social-emotional learning were critiques of the systemic inequities that continue to marginalize New Mexican students. For example, social-emotional learning emerged as an issue of access, as those students who needed the most support often had the least access to resources. Thus, analyzing and addressing systemic inequities was not only an ongoing component of our meetings and discussions but also an outgrowth of our writing process. The more we wrote, revisited, and revised our inquiry chapters, the more we were able to identify the various ways that educational, economic, and political systems inhibited our ability to teach and learn in ways that truly felt responsive to our students' needs.

A second critical theme that surfaced across chapters was the role of teacher activism in advocating for change. Many of us have participated in activist communities in Albuquerque (together and separately) as we worked to effect lasting change in New Mexico. *Teaching Out Loud* members have questioned administrators in public forums, burned teaching evaluations, attended rallies in support of public education, sent letters to state officials, created presentations to raise awareness among parents, organized conferences aimed at promoting critical consciousness among preservice teachers, and unabashedly taught critical content to foster more equitable spaces for students. These hxstories are recounted in our individual chapters and demonstrate the importance of collective will and collaboration. Even when we were not all participating in the same activist initiative, we supported one another as we navigated the tricky terrain of contesting dehumanizing practices in schools. In fact, many of us attribute *Teaching Out Loud* with being a collective that offered us hope and possibility during the darkest period of the pandemic. Our shared experiences of teaching over Zoom, supporting students through trauma, and sustaining our own emotional energy as we contended with increasingly bleak educational conditions provided us with motivation to continue.

Indeed, the difficulty of sustaining robust teacher inquiry work over time and space was another theme that surfaced across the chapters. As evidenced by our dynamic and ever-shifting group membership, people moved in and out of *Teaching Out Loud* according to their own individual capacities and their needs and priorities as educators. Some members left teaching altogether, some moved into master's programs in order to foster deeper intellectual growth, one member returned to teaching secondary school after several years away, and another took a semester-long sabbatical to participate in a Fulbright program. These shifting conditions are illustrative of the complexities and hardships that are endemic to teaching for the long term and the importance of committing to ongoing inquiry.

Teaching Out Loud is a place-based inquiry group intimately shaped by the unique cultural contours of New Mexico and the complex hxstories of the American Southwest. Yet we hope that in sharing the ways in which we mobilized one small group of educators and the learning and opportunities that surfaced as a result that we can inspire others to commit in substantive ways to making teacher research *in community* a part of their teaching practice. As with all inquiry practices, we recognize the work as unfinished and ongoing and acknowledge the importance of naming the questions that we will continue to carry forward into our individual and shared endeavors:

1. How can deep inquiry work by teachers be sustained over space and time?
2. How can inquiry groups be created and designed in ways that allow teachers to move in and out of them with fluidity to reflect teachers' shifting needs?
3. In what ways can teacher inquiry also support teacher agency and encourage educators to take a more active role in speaking back to dehumanizing policies and practices?
4. How can the work of teacher researchers be shared and publicized to audiences that are both invested in the local dimensions of the work and able to effect change on broader scales?

Together, *Teaching Out Loud* members explored issues related to race, gender, charter schools, sexuality, income inequality, curriculum, student-centered instruction, behavior and discipline, school reform, the corporate takeover of education, colonialism, culture and language, and mental health, among many others. We viewed these topics as absolutely essential to our daily classroom practice and at the heart of what it means to be teacher researchers.

About the Editors

Katherine Crawford-Garrett is an associate professor of teacher education, educational leadership, and policy at the University of New Mexico. She holds an EdD from the University of Pennsylvania as well as degrees from Middlebury College, Boston University, and Colgate University. Her areas of scholarship include neoliberal contexts of schooling, teacher activism, critical literacy, and feminism. She is the recipient of the 2016 Fulbright U.S. Scholar Award to study TeachFirst New Zealand, a program that prepares university graduates in New Zealand to work in high-poverty schools. She is the author of the book, *Teach for America and the Struggle for Urban School Reform* and a co-editor of the volume *Examining Teach for All: International Perspectives on a Growing Global Network* as well as articles in leading peer-reviewed journals such as the *American Educational Research Journal* and *Teaching and Teacher Education.*

Damon R. Carbajal (he/él) is a gay, queer Chicanx educator, scholar, and activist from Las Cruces, New Mexico. He holds a BA in secondary education, a minor in theatre, an MA in Chicana/o/x studies, and a graduate certificate in "Race" and Social Justice from the University of New Mexico. His research and activist work focuses on the experiences of LGBTQIA+ students and educators, mental health, and social justice. His work aims at recentering the lost voices in educational spaces with a focus on equity and social justice because he is a firm believer that all students and educators deserve to have their voice not only heard but centered. His work has been published in *The New Educator, Luminous Literacies: Localized Teaching and Teacher Education,* and *Chamisa Journal of Literary, Performance, and Visual Arts of the Greater Southwest.* ¡Sí Se Puede!

About the Contributors

Kristen Heighberger-Ortiz was born and raised in Cincinnati, Ohio, and has been teaching in Albuquerque for the past 25 years. Her experience spans private, parochial, and public schools in Grades K–3. She graduated from Bowling Green State University with a BS in elementary education and later received an ESL endorsement. In 2016, Ms. Heighberger-Ortiz became a National Board Certified teacher.

Linnea Holden (born and raised in New Mexico) has been working with small children for over 20 years as a babysitter, nanny, day care worker, after school program coordinator, and public school educator. She holds an ELL certificate and National Board Certification in early childhood education. She graduated from the University of New Mexico with a BA in social sciences and received her teaching license from the College of Santa Fe.

Amanda Y. Short has been both a special education and general education elementary school teacher with Albuquerque Public Schools for 15 years. She holds an ELL certificate and National Board Certification in middle childhood generalist education. She graduated from the University of New Mexico with a MA in special education. Ms. Short is a teacher-activist and is an advocate for teachers, parents, students, and public education. She was recently awarded a Fulbright Distinguished Award in Teaching, taking her to New Zealand, where she studied culturally responsive teaching practices.

Kahlil Simpson is a Black, biracial educator who teaches English and language arts at a public charter school in Albuquerque. He holds a master's degree in language, literacy, and sociocultural studies from the University of New Mexico. His work has been published in *Critical Education* and *The New Educator*.

Index